My Unknown Future

Rejuvenating Faith and Reliance in Allah

TRANSCRIBED AND ADAPTED FROM THE LECTURE
"MY UNKNOWN FUTURE: REJUVENATING FAITH AND
RELIANCE IN ALLAH"
BY
WAEL IBRAHIM

Published by:

Unit No. E-10, 5 Jln SS 15/4G, Subang Square,
47500 Subang Jaya, Selangor, Malaysia
+603-5612-2407 (office) / +6017-399-7411 (mobile)
info@tertib.press
www.tertib.press
@tertibpress (Facebook & Instagram)

Author	:	Wael Ibrahim
Transcriber & Editor	:	Arisha Mohd Affendy
Proofreader	:	Norashikin Azizan
		Nadiah Aslam
Cover designer	:	Abdul Adzim Md Daim
Typesetter	:	Abdul Adzim Md Daim

MY UNKNOWN FUTURE: REJUVENATING FAITH AND RELIANCE IN ALLAH

First Edition: May 2023

Contents

Preface

Assalamualaikum warahmatullahi wabarakatuh,

Bismillahirrahmanirrahim, *Allāhumma ṣalli ʿala sayyidina muḥammadin waʿala ali sayyidina muḥammad,* "O' Allah, send your blessings on Muḥammad and the progeny of Muḥammad."

The name *My Unknown Future* was selected beautifully, and it is related to me personally; two stories I will relate and I want you to forget who the person is in the story, and try to picture yourself about something else that happened in your life that led to the same outcome. Because how many of us have gone through a bad lifestyle before making a commitment to practise Islam? So if you now rewind that table of your history, and try to pinpoint the situations or the circumstances that makes you say, "You know what, this is the time to turn back to Allah (s.w.t.)." You will feel something strange, because when you are in the dark, when you are in those days, it seems like you own the world, it seems like things will remain the same forever. But actually things in the future are always unknown and uncertain.

Now this book will teach you on to be okay with uncertainty, because that is Islam basically. However, these things are not taught frequently, unfortunately.

So two stories just to give you an idea of why this is so special for me.

The first story started when I was back in those days, the 80s, 90s, when I was into music and singing. At that time, the idea of my future involved fame, money, travelling the world, getting my people running after me in the limelight, may Allah protect us all. Then an incident happened that changed my understanding of the future. It took me a period of depression, a period of sadness, a period of not accepting what had taken place in my life, which was not in my control. But after that incident, I started changing my idea of the future.

Yes, we want a lot of things to happen in the future, but it will not always happen the way that we want it to happen. That does not mean that we should not work for the future. Don't get me wrong. What I am trying to indicate here is that sometimes when we are in the process of planning our future, we forget our main objective of why we were created. And the *dunya* becomes the centre of our attention. *SubḥanAllāh*. Music, singing, fame, wealth, those were all *dunya*. What had happened was, all of a sudden, my role model, the singer that I looked up to, the singer that I was trying to compete with, commit suicide. That was the same man who had all the things that I wished for, and all of a sudden, he ended his life. What was even worse was the manner in which he ended his life, it was horrible. Back in his hotel room, he left a note that said 'depression'. So this just shows that money, fame, wealth, attention, media, all these things did not offer this man anything, except depression, and he died in it. *SubhanAllāh*. And it will not take us long to search few names on the internet who Allah bless them with the *dunya*, Allah gave them whatever they want, whatever they asked in the *dunya*, only for them to die committing suicide. William Robbins was one of them, he was a comedian actor, he made people laugh, but he was depressed.

So when we run after the *dunya*, this is what we are going to get. And that was the turning point that 'Oh the future that I used to look at is different', hence, my life regarding the *dunya* changed.

This is what this book is all about, our unknown future. What Allah (s.w.t.) destines us in the future is different, perhaps is far from what we are planning today. But the beauty of Islam, *Alhamdulillāh*, has taught us that no matter what happens to us in the future, we have to have *riḍa*—contentment. We have to be happy with Allah's (s.w.t.) destiny. So we can plan all we want, but if Allah (s.w.t.) has a different plan, we have to accept it.

The second story is about the book, 'My Wheelchair', my journey of how I got back on my feet. The story happened during the COVID-19 in 2020. I was washing my hands, as per the requirements and advice of the governments; 'Wash your hands regularly'. I was in the kitchen, between the toilet door and the sink, minding my own business, just washing my hands. Here is the thing though, when everybody understood the severity of my injury, they asked, "What did you do?", "What happened to you?". They want to hear some juicy stories like, "yeah, I was running" or "I'm with my car, and then there was a truck coming all the way, and the truck took me a few kilometres away, and my car flipped, like Fast & Furious, and this is why I lost my ability to walk.", they want to hear a big massive story, but the reality was, I was just washing my hands. How dangerous is that? How dangerous can washing hands be? All of a sudden, *wallahi,* I felt a crashing pain, that is the only description I can have for what happened to me on that day. Now before I tell you what happened next, prior to this minute, my future was to go to work the next morning. It was the first day of the new term I teach at school. And actually prior to going to that sink and wash my hands, I was preparing all my work for the next day. Did I think that in the next few minutes I would not be able to move even an inch?

This will be the discussion of this book, *Insha'Allāh.*

Because I believe we need to get back to the basics, if we don't, we will lose track of our direction. We will have all those depressive states. We see why all these mental severity, mental health affects us, just because we lost track of our directions. Allah (s.w.t.) said in the Qur'an:

$$\text{وَمَا خَلَقْتُ ٱلْجِنَّ وَٱلْإِنسَ إِلَّا لِيَعْبُدُونِ ﴿٥٦﴾}$$

"And I did not create the jinn and mankind except to worship Me."

(surah adh-Dhariyat, 51:56)

Our job in this *dunya* is to worship Allah (s.w.t.). Our title in this *dunya* is slave of Allah (s.w.t.). That is why Allah (s.w.t.) gave us surah al-Fatiḥah to remind us again and again:

$$\text{إِيَّاكَ نَعْبُدُ وَإِيَّاكَ نَسْتَعِينُ ﴿٥﴾}$$

"It is You we worship and You we ask for help"

(surah al-Fatiḥah, 1:5)

But sometimes we enslave ourselves to other things like money and desires. We want things according to our whims and wants, more than according to the will of Allah (s.w.t.),

5

and this is where we go wrong, this is where we lose our mind and directions as I mentioned earlier. If we do not get back on track, all these future plans of ours will get us nothing but depression. May Allah protect us all, 'amin.

So *SubhanAllāh*, I was washing my hands. A sudden crushing pain took me to the ground and pinned me there for a couple of hours. I tried to get up, as we always do when we fall down right? But every time I tried to move, a flaring pain went straight through my waist down. The screaming was loud, my wife was worried about the neighbours. I was screaming on top of my lungs, I was in pain, a pain that I have never experienced and I asked Allah (s.w.t.) never to give that sort of pain to anyone. *Wallah*, it was excruciating, the kind of pain where you would say, "I wish to die rather than experiencing the pain." Yes, I reached that state. And as we all know physical pain leads to emotional and mental pain. You cannot focus on anything else, you cannot do anything, you cannot function normally. *Wallahi*, it is terrible. May Allah ease our pain, *ya Rabb*.

I spent another three to four hours on the ground. Every time I tried to do anything, the pain would shoot everywhere in my body. *SubhanAllāh*, whenever that pain started, the mental pain started to strike as well. I started to feel the numbness going through my waist down. I can instantly feel certain parts of my leg became numb, but the pain is still there. Like your body is getting numb, but the pain is persisting. *Subḥan Allāh*, it was a very very difficult time. My wife ran to get some painkillers, and my children were trying to call the hospital. But the doctor could only come at five, and it was one at the time. My wife, may Allah bless her, and my daughter brought a blanket prior to the doctor's arrival, and they slowly put it under my body, and started dragging the blanket to the room, because I was still on the kitchen floor, and the place was very tight. Anyway, read the book if you want to know more, *Insha'Allāh*, I am not trying to make a sale, but read the book for the whole story because the book will give you that shift from the person's story to your story. That is the beauty, *Alḥamdulillāh*, that Allah blessed me with regarding this book. '*My Wheelchair*' becomes a symbol for all of us who are experiencing different sorts of pain and ways to cope with it, and how we can get back on track, *Insha'Allāh*.

But that was also another turning point for me about the future. At that time I was not a citizen in Australia yet, so my fear was that the school that I work with would tell me, "Sorry, you are useless now to us, so please go back to where you come from." And Hong Kong at that time was hectic due to COVID, people were leaving the city, going to the UK, giving up their citizenship. So where will I go now? My wife is from the Philippines, do I move there?

Even if I move to the Philippines, what am I going to do? So all that fear of the future striked and made me feel like I am a useless man. Until one man, may Allah bless him, Shaykh Haitham al-Haddad, one of the senior scholars of all time. He is from the UK, and *SubhanAllāh*, when he heard about my injury, he called me and I was complaining to the him, "Shaykh, I can't take it anymore, don't tell me to be patient." Shaykh Haitham al-Haddad told me, "You know my dear brother Wael, if your focus is on the pain, you will remain in pain, but if your focus is on the reward of the pain, you will gain the reward with Allah, and the pain will be subsided. So it's up to you my dear brother Wael, do you want the pain or do you want the reward of the pain?" "But it is excruciating Shaykh Haitham, you can't imagine." He said, "Well, the more painful your pain, the higher your reward. It's up to you."And he was so cool about it, he was the one who woke me up to reality. My future is going to be different, so I have to work according to that. This is when I discover what we are going to discuss about, if we are not actually aware about the Islamic principles, regarding our *deen* and the future ahead of us, *Jannah*, the Hereafter. And if we are stuck in this *dunya*, what will we even do? At the end of the day, where are we going to go in this *dunya*? We can accumulate money all we want, accumulate fame all we want, accumulate this *dunya*. Take it in, keep it in the bank, and keep everything all we want, because at the end of the day where are we going to leave all of that? On the earth, and we will be buried beneath the earth. That is the reality. So when we wake up to this reality, we have a choice now. What Allah (s.w.t.) said, and why Allah (s.w.t.) revealed in the Qur'an from above the seven heavens to save us and bring us to our senses, that this *dunya* is a place where we should work in preparation for *Jannah*.

The agenda that will be discussed:

1. What does it mean to be a Muslim?

What does it really mean to be a Muslim, and I don't want you to feel like, "O' brother, *Laillahaillah Muhammadur Rasulullah*, I want you to pay attention to everything we are going to say so then you can compare yourself just being a Muslim with being a Muslim—the real thing. And then tick the box, *Insha'Allāh*, if you need to modify something in your life, you are still breathing, you are still alive, so there is a possibility for us to still correct ourselves, *Insha'Allāh*.

2. The importance of actions in Islam.

There are people who have the idea that, "Since I said *Laillahaillah*, I'm going to *Jannah* anyway."

The Messenger of Allah (ﷺ) said, "He whose last words are: *La ilaha illallah* (There is no true god except Allah) will enter *Jannah*."

(Riyad as-Salihin 917)

So then we will enter *Jannah*, yes, but only after being punished for our sins. So depending on what we have done, we will still be punished. Be careful. Do not give ourselves that comfort of, "because I'm a Muslim, Hijabi, Niqabi from Malaysia, from Saudi, from Egypt I'm going to go to *Jannah* anyway." Do not have that confidence, ever. We will never enter *Jannah* with that attitude, not even with our actions. But are our actions important? Absolutely, yes. We will talk further about that soon, *Insha'Allāh*.

3. The nullifiers of iman/faith

What could you do, say, advice, introduce to your family members, introduce to your friends that could classify you as a *kafir*, that could take you outside the fold of Islam. Those are very dangerous things. And *Alḥamdulillāh*, in Islam we need to know the harmful things in order to avoid them.

"It was narrated from Thawban that the Prophet (ﷺ) said:

'I certainly know people of my nation who will come on the Day of Resurrection with good deeds like the mountains of Tihamah, but Allah will make them like scattered dust.' Thawban said: 'O Messenger of Allah, describe them to us and tell us more, so that we will not become of them unknowingly.' He said: 'They are your brothers and from your race, worshipping at night as you do, but they will be people who, when they are alone, transgress the sacred limits of Allah.'"

(Sunan ibn Majah, 4245)

Even though these people were of the higher level of mu'min, their actions were still not accepted by Allah (s.w.t.). They were of a higher level than us, they are not ordinary people. Yet, Allah (s.w.t.) will not accept their actions. What have they done? What is that one thing that nullifies their beliefs?

4. Returning to Allah

What can we do to return back to Allah (s.w.t.)? *Alḥamdulillāh*, so as long as we are breathing, Allah is giving us a chance to go back to Him. But if we keep saying, *Insha'Allāh*, brother just pray for me. We never know when will the angel of death come and say, "Hey, times up." May Allah protect us all.

5. Ath-Thabaat — steadfastness/ how to stick to your plan.

How can we maintain consistency? How can we remain firm and consistent? Consistency is actually the key to our success in this *dunya*. A quote from Denzel Washington 'Dreams without goals are just dreams.' So if we are dreaming of becoming something, but we do not have a target to reach, then they are just dreams. sIt will remain here in our mind, and it will disturb our peace. And he said that these dreams, these sort of dreams that are goalless, they will fuel disappointments. After 10 years you look back and said, "Oh, I haven't changed."

We will be disappointed, and start developing mental illnesses and whatnot. But then he said something very very important, he said, "Without commitment, you will never start anything." If we do not start committing on changing our lives forever now, *Insha'Allāh*, we will never start anything. We have to be committed, commit a promise to Allah from today onward, "this is what I'm going to do, *Insha'Allāh*." We have to have that intention, that we need to change, that we cannot be the same. He also said, "But most importantly, without consistency, you will never finish." We will remain the same. We will remain in the same place, stuck where we currently are.

So this is what we are going to do, *Insha'Allāh ta'ala*, as the agenda of the day. I hope and I pray that Allah (s.w.t.) will grant us all the right intention, and the energy to continue throughout the day, *bi iznillah* (with the will and permission of Allah).

Part 1:

What Does It Mean To Be A Muslim?

Allah says in the Qur'an:

$$\ldots\text{فَمَن يَكْفُرْ بِالطَّٰغُوتِ وَيُؤْمِنۢ بِٱللَّهِ فَقَدِ ٱسْتَمْسَكَ بِٱلْعُرْوَةِ ٱلْوُثْقَىٰ}\ldots ﴿٢٥٦﴾$$

"...So whoever disbelieves in ṭaghut and believes in Allāh has grasped the most trustworthy handhold with no break in it..."

(surah al-Baqarah, 256)

What is *taghut*? *Taghut* is anything being worshipped or favoured over Allah (s.w.t.) and His command. So anything that is being worshipped or favoured above Allah's commands and orders in the Qur'an or throughout the teaching of Prophet (s.a.w.) is called *taghut*. It is not a person. Some people think it is *Talut*, NO. *Taghut* is worshipping anything other than Allah (s.w.t.). So Allah is telling us here, "If you disbelieve in *taghut*, and believe in Allah (s.w.t.), then you will be successful, *insha'Allāh*. What does this mean my brothers and sisters? Please pay close attention to this. In order for us to really be classified as *mu'minin*, we have to be a disbeliever in some sense. In order for us to be classified and accepted as a *mu'minin*, we must—we have no option but to disbelieve, or to become a disbeliever in some things.

Otherwise, our *iman* will not be accepted. Can we be a complete *mu'minin*, a complete believer and celebrate an occasion which is classified as *khuruj* (exit—exiting Islam). Can we say "Merry Christmas" to the people next door because they are our neighbours and we want to appease and please them? Can we say "Happy Birthday" to the man who believes in a different God? "Congratulations, very happy for you that you have a God." Can we do that? No. However, that does not mean that we do not respect them as individuals. We should love our Christian neighbours. My entire family in-law are Christians, Catholics, and we all love each other. We converse, and we talk about religion all the time. But that does not mean that I will now hold everything dear to them as dear to me—because there are certain things, and certain limits that could actually put me in that category of the disbelievers. So I have to deny that part. "I can't have anything to do with this, sorry. My religion is asking me to only focus on Allah (s.w.t.)." That is why the Prophet (s.a.w.) said that there are only two *eids*, two festivals in our religion, which are *Eid al-Fitr* and *Eid al-Adha*. Very simple, and he said do not imitate any other groups who celebrate other celebrations.

"Anas ibn Malik reported:

The Messenger of Allah, peace and blessings be upon him, arrived in Medina during two days in which they were celebrating. The Prophet said, 'What are these two days?' They said, 'We would celebrate these two days in the time of ignorance.' The Prophet said, 'Verily, Allah has replaced these two days with two better days: *Eid al-Adha* and *Eid al-Fitr*.'"

(Sunan Abu Dawud 1134)

Do not come now and say, "But I think, but I believe, but I feel..." No. Allah (s.w.t.) already told us what to do, and what not to do, so do not say all of that, because that does not carry any weight in the eyes of Allah (s.w.t.). Our opinion does not matter. Who are we compared to the wisdom and knowledge of Allah (s.w.t.)?

So remember, in order for us to become a believer, we must neglect or leave behind any lifestyles that the Prophet (s.a.w.) did not bring to us. On the day of Judgement, the Prophet (s.a.w.) will be waiting for us at the pool where he will give us a drink that we will *Insha'Allāh* make us never feel thirsty. May Allah makes us among them, *'amin*.

"Narrated that Abu Haazim said: I heard Sahl say:

I heard the Prophet (s.a.w) say: 'I will reach the Cistern ahead of you. Whoever comes to it will drink and whoever drinks from it will never thirst again. Some people will come to me whom I will recognise and they will recognise me, but then a barrier will be placed between me and them.'"

(Bukhari 6528, Muslim 4243)

So he (s.a.w.) would be waiting for us, but in order for us to cross over to where he is, we have to pass through *as-Sirat*—the straight path. We always pray to Allah to guide us in this *dunya*, and the hereafter. Some people will cross like the wind, *Masha'Allāh*. And this *sirat* is not easy—it's very sharp like the edge of a sword, and very thin like a strand of a hair, and it has those hooks on its side that can catch you up and throw you off the bridge. May Allah (s.w.t.) protect us all.

Guide us to the straight path

(surah al-Fatiḥah, 1:6)

"...Abu Sa'id said: 'I have come to know that the bridge would be thinner even than the hair and sharper than the sword;...'"

(Ṣaḥiḥ Muslim 183b)

But for some people, some Muslims, they will be blocked from reaching the Prophet (s.a.w.). The angels will come and make a barrier between them and the Prophet (s.a.w.). But the Prophet (s.a.w.) will plead, "My *ummah*, my people, let them come through." Allah will say, "They are not your people. They are not your *ummah*. You don't know what they have done after you." May Allah protect us all.

"The Prophet (s.a.w.) said, I am your predecessor at the Lake-Fount (Kauthar) and some men amongst you will be brought to me, and when I will try to hand them some water, they will be pulled away from me by force whereupon I will say, 'O Lord, my companions!' Then the Almighty will say, 'You do not know what they did after you left, they introduced new things into the religion after you.'"

(Ṣaḥiḥ al-Bukhari 7049)

They have changed, some people have changed—they have adopted different ways of life. Life that the Prophet (s.a.w.) never brought to us. We look like Muslims, we talk like Muslims. How many of us have never said *insha'Allāh* today? How many of us have never said *alḥamdulillāh* today? We all have said it today, even when we are in pain or whenever we complain, *Masha'Allāh*. We will learn how to complain as well in this book. This is very essential. We should want to start the jorney of this book with these ground rules, that if we want to live according to our *iman* in Allah, we have to disbelieve and leave out other ways of lives that are not revealed by Him (s.w.t.), that we brought to ourselves. I want you all to imagine this with me. We are at home, doing whatever we are doing. Try to visualise it. A Friday night, the normal day to day activities in our home, and then all of a sudden, the door knocks, and we went to open the door and depends on the importance that we have been giving to the TV series or the songs, concert or famous people, we open the door and we find Prophet Muḥammad (s.a.w.). Will he like what we are doing? Will he (s.a.w.) actually set a foot in our house? A smoker came up to me once and said, "Brother, pray for me to quit smoking." I asked him, "Why can't you pray for yourself? Why don't you take this pack of cigarettes and a trash it in the bin?" "It's difficult," he said. "I know it's difficult, nothing is easy in this *dunya*."

The point is, life is uneasy. Yes, I will pray for all us but at the same time we have to do our part as well. I cannot just make a *du'a'* and for someone and wait for it to be accepted. There has to be actions as well. We have to do something too. So imagine doing all of these things and the Prophet (s.a.w.) is next to us. Will we tell the Prophet (s.a.w.) to do all of this? If the answer is no, then we must change. Start doing something that will make the Prophet (s.a.w.) comfortable to enter our home. May Allah protect us all.

CHAPTER 1:
CONDITIONS OF BEING A MUSLIM

CONDITION 1: TO DENY OTHER GODS

In order for us to be a true Muslim, we must deny other gods or other ways of life. We have to deny it completely. Before participating to a party invitation or movies, try asking all these questions;

Is it halal?

What is it about? What are we going to watch?

Who will be there?

Are there intermingling between sexes unnecessarily?

All these things are part of our day-to-day activities. There is a Shaykh of mine who said that, "If a day pass by from your life without asking if this is what you did, halal or haram, it means there is something wrong with your faith." Because it means that we do not care, we act impulsively. We do not think about whether what we are about to do is halal or haram. If we already know that it is halal, do it. Go for it. But if we are in doubt, we must ask, and reach out to people. We cannot just do it and say, *insha'Allāh* one day, I will change.

So we have to change, now. We have to do something different, *insha'Allāh*.

...ٱلْيَوْمَ أَكْمَلْتُ لَكُمْ دِينَكُمْ وَأَتْمَمْتُ عَلَيْكُمْ نِعْمَتِى وَرَضِيتُ لَكُمُ ٱلْإِسْلَـٰمَ دِينًا... ۝

"... This day I have perfected for you your religion and completed My favour upon you and have approved for you Islam as religion…"

(surah al-Maidah, 5:3)

Allah said, "This day I have perfected your religion for you", "Completed My favour upon you." Allah (s.w.t.) has completed this *deen* for us. We do not need to add anything to it because it is already perfect and complete. It is a whole. وَرَضِيتُ لَكُمُ ٱلْإِسْلَـٰمَ دِينًا, and "I have approved, I have accepted for you, this way of life." The life of Islam is the way of life that Allah (s.w.t.) will approve on the Day of Judgment. Allah (s.w.t.) says in another *ayah*:

وَمَن يَبْتَغِ غَيْرَ ٱلْإِسْلَـٰمِ دِينًا فَلَن يُقْبَلَ مِنْهُ وَهُوَ فِى ٱلْءَاخِرَةِ مِنَ ٱلْخَـٰسِرِينَ ۝

"And whoever desires other than Islam as religion - never will it be accepted from him, and he, in the Hereafter, will be among the losers."

(surah al-Imran, 3:85)

When we say Islam is the way, we have to now remind each other, what exactly is this way? How can we live in the way of Islam— in the proper way, in a manner that we will not also live in a Zombie land. I did not say we cannot watch TV. Watch anything you want, so long as you do not feed desires that will go against Allah's command. That's about it.

Islam is also not only about making us happy. Islam is not a psychiatric hospital. People go there to feel good. NO. Do not ever think that life is smooth, because life is not *Jannah*. If that is the conception of the world that we are living in—the *dunya*. Hence, we will then always be depressed. If we are working very hard to live a comfortable life, our life will end up being miserable, *wallahi*, believe me. Because life was never meant to be comfortable.

"We have certainly created man into hardship."

(surah al-Balad, 90:4)

Allah said in surah al-Balad, "We created man to live in this *dunya* in a continuous state of toil and struggle." That is your life.

$$\text{أَحَسِبَ ٱلنَّاسُ أَن يُتْرَكُوٓا۟ أَن يَقُولُوٓا۟ ءَامَنَّا وَهُمْ لَا يُفْتَنُونَ ۝}$$

"Do the people think that they will be left to say, 'We believe' and they will not be tried?"

(surah al-Ankabut, 29:2)

Do people think that just because they said "We believe", they will be left to themselves doing whatever they wish without being tested? NO. We will be tested just like how the people before us were tested. Why? To filter the truthful, the honest, and the most genuine people from the liars and the hypocrites. Allah wants to filter those people because *Jannah* is not cheap. The Prophet (s.a.w.) said:

$$\text{...إِنَّ سِلْعَةَ اللَّهِ غَالِيَةٌ أَلَا إِنَّ سِلْعَةَ اللَّهِ الْجَنَّةَ...}$$

26

"...the commodity of Allah is precious. Verily the commodity of Allah is *Jannah*..."

(Riyad as-Salihin 410)

So we have to do our part. We have to work hard, and avoid every tempting moments. For instance, how many of us during Ramadan, look at a cold glass of water and salivate, or while walking down the streets in the midday of Ramadan, and see a non Muslim passing by with a delicious ice cream, and say, "*Allahumma inni saa'im* (O' Allah, I am fasting." Ramadan is a beautiful month. That is why the best and the most beloved act of worship in the side of Allah is fasting. That is the one act where people do not know whether we are fasting or not. It is an act of worship that we can cheat very easily, and nobody will know it, it is between us and Allah (s.w.t.). That is why it is beloved. And it is the only month that trains us on the reality of the *dunya*. The only act of worship in Islam that trains us continuously every day for thirty days. This is the reality of the *dunya*. Do not run after desires. Do not run after what we really want. Those who choose desires over what Allah has revealed in Qur'an, they are classified as worse than animals. What is my evidence? Allah (s.w.t.) told us in the Qur'an:

وَلَقَدْ ذَرَأْنَا لِجَهَنَّمَ كَثِيرًا مِّنَ ٱلْجِنِّ وَٱلْإِنسِ ۖ لَهُمْ قُلُوبٌ لَّا يَفْقَهُونَ بِهَا وَلَهُمْ أَعْيُنٌ لَّا يُبْصِرُونَ بِهَا وَلَهُمْ ءَاذَانٌ لَّا يَسْمَعُونَ بِهَآ ۚ أُو۟لَٰٓئِكَ كَٱلْأَنْعَٰمِ بَلْ هُمْ أَضَلُّ ۚ أُو۟لَٰٓئِكَ هُمُ ٱلْغَٰفِلُونَ ﴿١٧٩﴾

"And We have certainly created for Hell many of the jinn and mankind. have hearts with which they do not understand, they have eyes with which they do not see, and they have ears with which they do not hear. Those are like livestock; rather, they are more astray. It is they who are the heedless.

(surah al-A'raf, 7:179)

Allah has created *Jahannam* for people and the *jinn*. Why? لَهُمْ قُلُوبٌ لَّا يَفْقَهُونَ بِهَا, because they have got the hearts, the intellect, but they do not use it in their favour. They have got the eyes, they can see the signs. They can see people dying every day, but they do not pay heed. They have the ears, and they hear the reminders. How many Fridays we have attended and we never applied what has been said in the *khutbah*? How many lectures of that time we have attended and we went just like, *MashāAllāh*, it was so beautiful. What was it about? "I don't really know, but it was very beautiful."

So Allah is mentioning those people, that because of the faculties, the functions that Allah gave us and we are not using it in our favour, those people are like animals. Allah said in the same *ayah*, أُوْلَـٰئِكَ كَٱلْأَنْعَـٰمِ بَلْ هُمْ أَضَلُّ , those are like cattle, like animal, and then He said, no they are even worse, أُوْلَـٰئِكَ هُمُ ٱلْغَـٰفِلُونَ, those are the heedless people. Those are the heedless people who wish for things to happen on their own magically. For example, they say "*InshàAllāh* I'll change someday, when I get married, *InshàAllāh*," but then they do not change themselves into being a better person, characcter wise or health wise. "*InshàAllāh* brother, I will quit smoking next Ramadan. So I'll keep smoking for one year until Ramadan comes", and before Ramadan, he passes away. And so we will never know when our time will come.

So seize this opportunities to create the necessary change. Allah's *deen* is perfect. That is it. Don't add, don't extract. Don't bring our opinion into the matter. It's none of our business.

CONDITION 2: TO WORSHIP ALLAH WITH COMPLETE DEVOTION AND SINCERITY

The second condition is to worship Allah (s.w.t.) with complete devotion and sincerity for His sake, because we know and we trust that His *deen* has been made complete for us. We do not need to add anything.

$$إِنَّآ أَنزَلْنَآ إِلَيْكَ ٱلْكِتَـٰبَ بِٱلْحَـقِّ فَٱعْبُدِ ٱللَّهَ مُخْلِصًا لَّهُ ٱلدِّينَ ۝$$

"Indeed, We have sent down to you the Book, [O Muḥammad], in truth. So worship Allah, [being] sincere to Him in religion."

(surah az-Zumar, 39:2)

Our job, as mentioned earlier, is to worship Allah (s.w.t.) with a complete certainty—pure sincerity, pure heart. That is why Allah mention in this *ayah*:

$$قُلْ إِنَّ صَلَاتِى وَنُسُكِى وَمَحْيَاىَ وَمَمَاتِى لِلَّهِ رَبِّ ٱلْعَـٰلَمِينَ ۝$$

"Say, 'Indeed, my prayer, my rites of sacrifice, my living and my dying are for Allāh, Lord of the worlds.'"

(surah al-An'am, 6:162)

Tell them, "O' Muhammad (s.a.w.) that my prayer—the five days prayers that we perform every day and night, including the sunnah prayers and the *du'a's, hajj* and all the other rituals that were introduced by the Prophet (s.a.w.), but the final two points are amazing, my entire life, all those years that we are here on earth, even the moment of my death, I have dedicated that and I have given that to Allah (s.w.t.)." Can we imagine, every minute that we live on earth, we have to remind ourselves that this step that we are walking towards is for Allah's sake.

Ask ourselves, "What does it mean to you to do anything for the sake of Allah?" Because we heard this a lot, "I love you for the sake of Allah.", or "Do it for the sake of Allah." *Fī sabīlillāhi.* But what does that really mean to us?

Look at the *ayah* again, Allah is informing His messenger that our *salah*, our *'ibadah*, our entire rituals and life, even our death—even when we come to die before Allah (s.w.t.), it should be given completely for the sake of Allah. That is who we are. Unless we understand this reality, the *dunya* will steal us, which if we want it, Allah can give it to you from A to Z. However, if we want *Jannah*, if our ultimate goal is *al-Akhirah*, Allah will give *al-Firdaus* and this *dunya*, without you even running after it. Without even planning it, Allah will open doors because perhaps the intention was Allah and Allah alone.

CONDITION 3: TO PRACTISE ISLAM WHOLEHEARTEDLY

Number 3 is to practise Islam wholeheartedly, no picking, no choosing. How many of us sisters have struggled to put hijab on? And I can guarantee us that the following statement was a part of our life. Like, *"Insha'Allāh, when I am totally convinced, then I will."*

There was a Catholic nun in the Philippines who embraced Islam, and it took her a while to put her hijab on. Before Islam, she used to wear veil, bandeau and a coif, so she used to wear hijab better than many Muslims in the sense of covering her body. However, when she became a Muslim, she started wearing those short skirts, and removed her scarf. Then, we took her to a Shaykh for a brief discussion, and he told her, *"Masha'Allāh*, sister you came here to embrace Islam?" She said, "No, I became a Muslim two years ago, *Masha'Allāh*. I was a Catholic nun." He said, *"Masha'Allāh*, so where is your hijab?" The Shaykh was so direct, there was no joke about it. She said, "Brother, hijab is in my heart." You know what the Shaykh said? He said, "Take it out from your heart and put it on your head."

How many of us sometimes feel like they do not want to pray because they have a fight with someone, and they are very angry? They would say, "I will pray later, because my heart is not connected right now." How many of us have felt that before? That is *shaytan*. One of the greatest traps of *shaytan* is to get us into a fight with somebody else, like a husband and wife. Those who are married, they experience a little bit of annoyance with their spouses sometimes. This is in every home. I heard some saying, "Brother, I have not been praying, I can't focus on my prayer, because I fight with my wife all the time." This is the problem when the *dunya* takes us away from the main purpose of why we were created. A fight with your wife prevented you from worshipping Allah. And the Prophet (s.a.w.) said, "*Salah* is the backbone of the *deen*."

So if anything happens to that backbone of the *deen*, then what will happen to the entire religion? It demolishes. ومـن أقـام الصـلاة فقـد أقـام الديـن, whosoever established *salah*, established the *deen*. و مـن تركها فقـد هـدم الدين, and whosoever demolished *salah*, has demolished the *deen* of Allah (s.w.t.). So *salah* is very important. So be careful, do not let *shaytan* take us away from our purpose in life because of this *dunya*. So we have to practise them without picking and choosing, without saying "*InshàAllāh*, later." NO. Just do it. And then Allah will open doors for us to accept the practice and become part of our existence.

We are talking to a person who used to wake up during *maghrib* time and sleep during *fajr*. That was my day and night. I never thought one day will come that I will wake up for *fajr* to pray and then sleep early so that I can wake up early the next day. So Allah created us with the ability to change. My wife lived almost all her life as a Catholic Christian, who could have believed that one day she would change. I married her when she was a Catholic, she told me one day, "I don't want you to discuss with me about religion anymore. You know I love Jesus, Jesus is my saviour. So I feel like if I continue this, I would be betraying Jesus." She went from that to أَشْهَـدُ أَنْ لَا إِلٰه اِلَّا الـلّٰه, to Islam, to *shahadah*, with tears. Even going her way to invite her family to Islam. Who could have done that change? Allah (s.w.t.). So Allah (s.w.t.) can change us, but only if we can take a step.

$$...إِنَّ ٱللَّهَ لَا يُغَيِّرُ مَا بِقَوْمٍ حَتَّىٰ يُغَيِّرُوا۟ مَا بِأَنفُسِهِمْ...$$

"…Indeed, Allah will not change the condition of a people until they change what is in themselves…"

(surah ar-Rad, 13:11)

Allah will not just simply send angels to change us, we must take that step—one baby step—towards that change, and Allah will do the rest, *insha'Allāh*.

يَـٰٓأَيُّهَا ٱلَّذِينَ ءَامَنُوا۟ ٱدْخُلُوا۟ فِى ٱلسِّلْمِ كَآفَّةً وَلَا تَتَّبِعُوا۟ خُطُوَٰتِ ٱلشَّيْطَـٰنِ ... ﴿٢٠٨﴾

"O' you who have believed, enter into Islām completely [and perfectly] and do not follow the footsteps of Satan."

(surah al-Baqarah, 2:208)

Allah (s.w.t.) said enter into Islam wholeheartedly. We cannot become a Muslim partially or becoming a part-time Muslim. If we do, Allah will question us. In the *ayah*, He said, "and be careful, do not follow the footsteps of *shaytan*." Because *shaytan* will not come and say, "hey, let's go and do *zina*." *Shaytan* does not actually advise us directly to do the haram, but they will pull our legs slowly. Starting with unnecessary conversations, chatting with different gender. for instance or husbands who are chatting with other females unnecessarily—there is no reason why the conversation is taking place, other than them just liking the hype. They are married, and they are hurting their spouse. It makes them feel jealous, it makes them feel that there is something going on. So wake up. If there is a business, if it is business related, then converse in public, do it in the open. But if there is nothing, no business, be careful. If we are single, then it is even worse. We are chatting, and then chatting will turn into, "I wish to see you one day." And sometimes it begins with hijab, like chatting with a haram brother in hijab. Later on, when you started becoming accustomed to the conversations, you will then start getting used to each other. That is how our brain works. Our brain learns from our actions, just like addictions. In the beginning you are actually shivering, you are scared. Your heart is pumping too fast. "Aḥmad is coming, Aḥmad is coming." Once Aḥmad becomes normal, then every day you are chatting with Aḥmad, your brain becomes desensitised. Then Aḥmad one day will tell you, "I wish to see if your hair is long or short." And before you know it, there is more than just the reveal of the hair happening. May Allah protect us all. So, be careful.

This is *khuṭuwatu shayṭan* (*shayṭan*'s steps). Slowly but surely we will fall, if we do not avoid evil from its root. If we do not cut it from its root, it will grow and it will get a hold of us. If you do not believe me, read the story of the priest, which the Prophet (s.a.w.) mentioned about who was known for his excellent worship. He had neighbours, three brothers and a sister. Those three brothers were called for war, and they entrusted their sister with that priest who they thought was a religious man whom could protect their sister. But because he did not avoid *khuṭuwatu shayṭan*, *shayṭan* came and told him, "hey, you have been putting the food every day on the door without even knowing whether she is alive or not. Just knock the door, hear her voice." He followed *shaytan* and she responded, "Yes?" And that is how he got attracted to the sound. How many of us sometimes dial the wrong number? Especially the brothers. And some sister pick up the phone and respond in a voice that makes you go, 'WOW'. And you imagine in your brain how she looks like if her voice is like that. Continuing with the story, the *shaytan* commented, "maybe open the door just to make sure that she's okay, that she has eaten what you gave her." At last, he saw her, and she was beautiful. *Shaytan* then said, "sit down now, eat and talk together and chat with each other, and see if she needs more help. Now close the door, because people might think that you are doing something haram." Look at what *shaytan* did, now the door is closed, and behind the closed door, anything can happen. She then got pregnant, and she delivered the baby. But because the man is known for his worship and righteousness, he killed her and the baby, and buried her in her house, under the bed. When the brothers showed up, he told them that she got a disease and died, and he buried her somewhere, and he forged a grave. Look at *shaytan*, how many crimes have been committed because of that one small push. And at the end of the story, Allah (s.w.t.) showed a dream to the three brothers that their sister and her son were buried beneath them. They woke up relayed the dream to one another, they dug under their bed, and they found the two bodies. They exposed the man, and he was put on trial, and was executed. At the time of the execution, *shaytan* came to him—*shaytan* will never give up on us. He is very dedicated with his job to mislead us from the path of Allah (s.w.t.) with his tricks. So *shaytan* said, "I got you into this trouble, and I am the only one who can get you out of it." "Okay, what do I do?", the man asked. "Prostrate to me.", said the *shaytan*. So it is not only about crimes now, it is turning into *shirk*. The unforgivable sin. So the man prostrated, and as he was prostrating, they chopped off his head, and he died, in *shirk*. Why? Because of *khutuwatu shaytan*.

So always ask yourself;

Where are you going?

What is the nature of this conversation?

Why am I doing this?

Is there any benefit?

Is there any halal or haram?

Even if you intend to marry, you want to get married, *alhamdulillāh*, it is the best thing you can do. Because it will curb the desires, and it will prevent us from going to this haram websites that are available by the billions. If I give you the statistics, you will be going crazy yourself. So get married, *insha'Allāh ta'ala*. But even about getting married, we have to do it in the right way. We cannot just go outside holding hands, or even chat behind closed doors. No, there must be someone monitoring the conversations until, *insha'Allāh*, things turn serious and then get married, and live a halal life. Because if we are drown in haram, Allah will never even accept our *du'a'*. Remember, if we are nourishing ourselves in haram, Allah will not even accept our *du'a'*. So may Allah (s.w.t.) grant us the right understanding. That is why Allah (s.w.t.) said:

$$...\text{إِخْرَاجُهُمْ ۚ أَفَتُؤْمِنُونَ بِبَعْضِ ٱلْكِتَـٰبِ وَتَكْفُرُونَ بِبَعْضٍ ۚ} ... ۝٨٥$$

...So do you believe in part of the Scripture and disbelieve in part?...

(surah al-Baqarah, 2:85)

Do you believe in one part of the Qur'an and reject the rest? There are some sisters who got scared of the word polygamy. There are no sister that I came across that would say, "Oh, polygamy is very nice, let's do it." All sisters here, they have some fear, even those who accept, perhaps they say,

"Oh, I accept, I have a co-wife." But in general, sisters will have some fear, and it is understandable. Even the not being able to live in such relationship is also understandable. Like if your husband come and say, "I intend to marry again, I can't take it, I won't be able to function normally." You start feeling like your mental health is being affected. It is going to get worse and worse, if your husband just went ahead with his decision and marry a second wife. It is going to be devastating for the first wife as she cannot cope with such a lifestyle. So it is okay to say "I can't cope with polygamy." But if you say, "I don't accept polygamy at all", you are actually rejecting the Qur'an. If you say, "Oh, I hate this kind of relationship.", and start looking at polygamy as something evil, you are telling Allah that you are not wise enough, *astagfirullāh*.

So there is a fine difference between those two, there are things that we cannot practise. That is okay, because we are human beings, we have certain abilities and capacities. But not accepting anything that is revealed in the Qur'an or through the Prophet (s.a.w.), is the area of *kufr*. May Allah protect us all.

CHAPTER 2:
DEFINITION OF ISLAM

Islam is a beautiful word. The root word of Islam is س-ل-م (S-L-M), which amazingly means more than actually what we are going to discuss. But these are the five main things about Islam. It means submission to the will of Allah (s.w.t.). Ask ourselves, "Am I now following Allah in doing what I'm about to do, or am I going against Allah's will and doing the will of my own desire?"

The second is surrender—to give up. Giving up all the haram for the sake of Allah (s.w.t.). That is surrender. "I don't want to do this anymore, I don't want to talk to Ahmad anymore. I will send a last message saying, 'Listen up, if you are interested in *nikah*, marriage, here is my father's number.'" Simple. And if you are Ahmad, man up, and go get married. *Wallah*, man up. Do not waste your time sitting in your room, talking to sister Khadija online just to fuel your desire, and to feed that wolf in you. Because what is it that you are talking about? If you have no intention, no planning on your unknown future, then you are doing haram. I guarantee you 110%. Now you say, "Oh brother, you don't know the future." "I know."

They come to me for counselling after the problem is happening. That is why I have that confidence that if you have no conversation about marriage, if you are not involving parents or adults in your circle to monitor that conversation, you are doing haram. Whatever the level of haram, in Islam there are major and minor sins. But when Prophet (s.a.w.) spoke about minor sins, which we usually look at trivially, like white lies. Why is it called white? It is to indicate PURE. Can we imagine a lie, the most hateful thing in the side of the Prophet (s.a.w.) became pure—the symbol of purity is given. In Islam there are no white, black, or even purple lies. Lies are lies. There are three conditions in which a muslim may alter wrong information.

Three situations in which a muslim may lie;

1. In the time of war, when you want to mislead your enemies.

2. To reconcile between two people who are quarrelling. So you say a few nice words that are not necessarily true, but to melt the hearts and reconcile.

3. Between husband and wife. Uttering sweet words between husband and wife even if you exaggerated a little bit.

Only in these three situations did the Prophet (s.a.w.) allowed wrong information to be mentioned.

"It is not lawful to lie except in three cases: Something the man tells his wife to please her, to lie during war, and to lie in order to bring peace between the people."

(Jami` at-Tirmidhi 1939)

And we can measure that one other situation like, going to a friend's baby party, we look at the baby and went, "Oh my, why does the baby look like that?" So from our perspective the baby does not look as cute as our standard. Now imagine if our best friend comes to us and ask, "What do you think about my new baby?" We cannot just say, "*Masha'Allāh*, so ugly." So we have to say a few nice words to make the mother happy. These are the only conditions, no other lies are acceptable in Islam. Nothing. Even if that lie will cause us some harm in this *dunya*. We have to see the truth.

Next, we have obedience. One of the top definition is obedience, Allah (s.w.t.) in the Qur'an, the last two *ayah* of surah al-Baqarah, that is often recited, He (s.w.t.) is describing the believers, He says, "Those believers when the commands are revealed to them—when they are told what is halal and what is haram, وَقَالُوا سَمِعْنَا وَأَطَعْنَا, they said, 'we hear and we obey'," That is our job—to obey, because obedience is a part of Islam.

And remember, when we hear someone of knowledge telling us to be careful and what we are doing is haram. Even if the act from our perspective does not harm other people. Have you seen those people, the brothers especially, have this haircut where they shaved their hair on both sides of his head and left only the middle part. This haircut is called *al-qaza'*, and there is a ḥadith mentioned where the Prophet (s.a.w.) defined al-*al-qaza'*, as to cut parts of your hair and to leave the rest, and he (s.a.w.) prohibited such a haircut.

"The Messenger of Allah [SAW] forbade Al-Qaza'
(to shave part of the head and leave part)."

(Sunan an-Nasa'i 5051)

Now some people may ask "why?" Do we sometimes have that curiosity to ask why? Okay, here is the thing, how many of us has been to *hajj* or *umrah*, the Ka'bah? How many of us are able to kiss the black stone? Why do we kiss the black stone? Why do we have to kiss any stone in the first place? The reason is, we kissed the black stone because we saw the Prophet (s.a.w.) kissed the black stone. That is the only reason, whether that reason make sense to us or not, that is Islam—submission. Will we doubt the Prophet (s.a.w.)?

Abbas bin Rabi'ah said:

"I saw Umar bin Al-Khattab kissing the (Black) Stone and saying: 'I am kissing you while I know that you are just a stone, and if I had not seen the Messenger of Allah kissing you, I would not kiss you.'"

(Jami` at-Tirmidhi 860)

So this is Islam. It is to actually act out of complete trust, even if the action goes against our common sense, because we are not as wise as Allah (s.w.t.). We will never come to that level.

There was another incident where Prophet (s.a.w.) was leading a *salah* in one of the battles, and he was praying in his shoes, so all of the companions behind him were in shoes during the *salah*. The Prophet was leading the *salah* calmly as usual, very firm and focused, all of a sudden, he removed his shoes while praying. He did not tell anyone anything, he simply just removed his shoes quietly. Guess what happened behind him. All of the companions started removing their shoes.

"While the Messenger of Allah (ﷺ) was leading his Companions in prayer, he took off his sandals and laid them on his left side; so when the people saw this, they removed their sandals. When the Messenger of Allah (ﷺ) finished his prayer, he asked: What made you remove your sandals?

They replied: 'We saw you remove your sandals, so we removed our sandals'…"

(Sunan Abi Dawud 650)

So I want all of us to think of that scenario, if I took of my shoes and everybody else started following me, then after we finished our *salah*, logically speaking, who should ask 'why did you remove your shoe?' and to who? Should the Prophet ask the companions, or the other way around? The companions should ask the Prophet (s.a.w.), that is the logic, because he started the action. However, all of the companions, without exception, zipped their mouths. No one dared to open their mouths. The Prophet (s.a.w.) asked them the question instead. And they answered, "we saw you removing them, so we removed them." They did not even have the curiosity that kills us today. Because they have that full trust in the man that he is the prophet of Allah. If any, مَـا يَنطِـقُ عَـنِ ٱلْهَـوَىٰ, he does not speak or do anything out of his own will and desire, إِنْ هُـوَ إِلَّا وَحْـيٌ يُوحَـىٰ, whatever he is doing, his entire life is a revelation from Allah (s.w.t.). So how could we doubt the man? If there is a reason, he will give it to us, he will tell us why. There must be a reason, but some reasons we do not need to know. That is why Allah said in the Qur'an also to avoid these questions, if the answers are made clear to us, it will hurt us. It will make our life

48

miserable, like going to the *masjid*, some people have those doubts—*waswas*, and they step upon the streets and water seep inside their shoes, they look at their shoes and started questioning, "is this a *najis*? Is it dirty? Is it a urine?", so they leave the *masjid*, the *salah*, and they go back home to change, and by the time they are done, the prayer is over.

يَـٰٓأَيُّهَا ٱلَّذِينَ ءَامَنُوا۟ لَا تَسْـَٔلُوا۟ عَنْ أَشْيَآءَ إِن تُبْدَ لَكُمْ تَسُؤْكُمْ... ۝

"O' you who have believed, do not ask about things which, if they are shown to you, will distress you…"

(surah al-Ma'idah, 5:101)

So try to go into details, why do we do the seven circumambulations around the Ka'bah, not seven and a half? Why do we all go to Makkah during *hajj*? Those who have went to *hajj*, have you experienced the difficulty of *tawaf ul wada*? The farewell *tawaf*? It feels like you are actually not walking, people behind you are pushing you. But you did it anyway, for three hours one round, why is that? Because this is the way it was done by the best of all creation. And I am following his footsteps because these footsteps will lead me to the same destination, *Insha'Allāh*, which is *Jannah*.

So that is Islam brothers and sisters, we have to now dig into our lives and tick those boxes, like 'what needs to be eliminated that will displease Allah and His Messenger?' 'what will actually bring us closer to them in general?'

Number four is sincerity. Be careful, because this is the element that can define our action, whether it is acceptable by Allah (s.w.t.) or not. So any actions that we do has to be sincerely for the sake of Allah (s.w.t.). What does it mean to do anything for the sake of Allah? One sister said that it is so that Allah can love her for what she did in return. That is partially beautiful. Doing the things for the sake of Allah means when we pray, we do not expect anything in return from any human beings. When we recite the Qur'an beautifully, we are not doing it because we want people to come and say, "*Masha'Allāh* brother, your voice is nice." We are coming all the way for *da'wah* not because so that people will appreciate us, *wallahi*.

I had a shaykh of mine, may Allah bless him wherever he is, we invited him in Hong Kong, and this man if I told you his name, and you go search his name, you will see that he is one of the top senior scholars from Egypt. Who rise to the pulpit in the year 1970s, he is a student of Abdul Hamid Kishk, another giant shaykh from Egypt who I think senior Malaysian know these people, like very heavyweight scholars. And *SubḥanAllāh* because of his sharp tongue about the governments during Abdul Nasseer and Sadat, prisons here and there, he was forced to leave the country, but he did not stop his *da'wah*. He went to so many places, and he ended up in Hong Kong for, *SubhanAllāh*, two years. And this is how blessed I was during the time to learn first hand from that shaykh. I do not want to mention his name for some security reason. But the point is, this mess, *SubhanAllāh*, we invited him to give lecture to the Arab community, because this guy will filled up the venue simply because his name is very popular among the Arabs. When he went to Tunisia during the revolution, 200 000 attended his lectures. Then, he ended up in Hong Kong and we arranged the event, we prepared a table and chair for the shaykh to sit, and the volunteers were going crazy, because thirty minutes after the time that was allocated for the lecture, nobody showed up. An hour and a half later, this shaykh was still sitting in his seat, but he never even signal to us. What is happening? *Wallahi*, he was just sitting with his notes. And then we finally decided to cancel the event. One of my best friend who was always the one who pushed me towards an uncomfortable positions, like he was the one who pushed me towards studying bachelor degree Islamic studies with him, but then he left. So this friend of mine told me, "Go tell him, he listens to you, you invited him for us, and you discover that he is coming to Hong Kong, so you go." So I said to the shaykh, "*Assalamualaikum* shaykh, *wallahi* I don't know where to start, I am really really sorry, but we have to call the event off because unfortunately nobody shows up. I don't know why, probably there is something outside the trains, maybe there is a big accident happening." So yeah, I tried to invent any stories in my brain because I am so ashamed. You know what he said? He said, "*Allāhu akbar wa lillāhil ḥamd.*" And I was like, "Shaykh please, I'm sorry.", and then all of a sudden, "*Allāhu akbar wa lillāhil ḥamd.*", so I looked at him and said, "No, I think you misunderstood." So he said again, "*Allāhu akbar wa lillāhil ḥamd.*", I said, "for what?", like what are you celebrating? He said, "because now I can go back to the hotel and sleep, with my reward full because I did not come for the people." Meaning of course I come to educate you, but I did not come for you so that I can gain the reward from Allah (s.w.t.). You are not in that picture. And in my calculation, people are important in the sense that they received the knowledge and act upon it, and that is their job, their thing. Now you will be responsible for everything you learn today, not me. I already did my part. And as for the reward, I am not waiting on anyone to tell me thank you. Nothing. That should be the attitude, that is sincerity.

So whatever we do, remember, do not expect anything in return from the people, expect all the rewards and all the goodness from Allah (s.w.t.). So when we tell somebody "I love you for the sake of Allah." What does that mean? It means, "I love you despite your Mercedes, or your bank account. I do not care about that. I love you for the sake of Allah." And if that happens, guess what? Allah will love us for this.

And finally peace. So Islam does not mean peace by the way. If we want to take a side note, peace is the result of being a pure and truesome. So that is the part that will solve the problem of our future. Like whatever happen in our future that we are unaware of, we will receive it with a calm and peaceful heart. Peace within ourselves, peace with the people around us, and peace with Allah before anyone else. So when we fight, we will feel angry internally, but our reaction will be the acceptable act towards Allah (s.w.t.).

Back in the days, I remember, when it rains, I will get very angry. Not only that, I will become very abusive if I am driving in Egypt. So we drive the car, and once it rains in Egypt, there would be traffics, and it will be muddy, and everybody is running, trying to get to where they want, and that makes everybody at rage. So if somebody cut me off, my waist would come out of the car window to abuse the person who cut me off. Yes, we snap sometimes, even until now, but the general practice is that we should behave in a manner that would be pleasing to Allah (s.w.t.).

A side note, the Prophet (s.a.w.) was burying his own son, Ibrahim, and he was in tears. He was so sad that his beloved son just died, may Allah (s.w.t.) ease the hearts of those who have lost their children or parents or anyone for that matter. *Amin ya rabbal a'lamin.* But look at the behaviour of the Prophet (s.a.w.), he was laying his son in the grave, weeping and crying, to an extent that a companion said, "The Prophet of Allah is crying?" Like he can cry? He was the one who taught us patience, so why is he crying? So he said, "It's the mercy from Allah to cry, otherwise you will burst, explode."

How many of us have heard some people trying to comfort someone by telling them not to cry or not to be sad? Imagine you have lost someone you truly care about, and you are sad, but people just said, "Do not be sad." Do we have an application to alter our emotions, from being sad to being happy? The Prophet (s.a.w.) was very sad and in tears. Not only that, but he was broadcasting the scene. Nobody talks like that, except for the Prophet of Allah. The Prophet said, إِنَّ الْعَيْنَ تَدْمَعُ, "Indeed, my eyes are shedding tears." He was broadcasting. This is the way Prophet (s.a.w.) coped with his sadness, an emotion that was intense for him at that moment. وَالْقَلْبَ يَحْزَنُ, "And my heart is shattered—my heart is grieving." But then he said something, the solution to anyone, "But we only say what is pleasing to Allah (s.w.t.)."

إِنَّـا لِلَّهِ وَإِنَّـا إِلَيْـهِ رَاجِعُـونَ, "And we belong to Allah, and to Him we shall return." So cry all you want, express your emotions all you want, in a manner that is pleasing to Allah.

Narrated Anas bin Malik:

We went with Allah's Messenger (ﷺ) (p.b.u.h) to the blacksmith Abu Saif, and he was the husband of the wet-nurse of Ibrahim (the son of the Prophet). Allah's Messenger (ﷺ) took Ibrahim and kissed him and smelled him and later we entered Abu Saif's house and at that time Ibrahim was in his last breaths, and the eyes of Allah's Messenger (ﷺ) (p.b.u.h) started shedding tears. `Abdur Rahman bin `Auf said, "O Allah's Apostle, even you are weeping!" He said, "O Ibn `Auf, this is mercy." Then he wept more and said, "The eyes are shedding tears and the heart is grieved, and we will not say except what pleases our Lord, O Ibrahim! Indeed we are grieved by your separation."

(Ṣaḥiḥ al-Bukhari 1303)

Now *Alhamdulillāh,* I came to a peaceful decision within myself that I would not allow anyone to come and try to alter my emotions. And I learned that during the time of my wheelchair incident, people will come and say, "hey, man up, toughen up a bit." I will be crying, my tears were flowing because of the pain, and some people would say something like, "come on, man don't cry." When I first started practising Islam, I went to a *masjid* for the first time, looking for somebody to teach me, and I found some Egyptian like me. So, when Egyptians meet one another, they are very noisy. So when I met him, I was excited, we hugged and kissed each other. And then, a man came from afar with his finger pointing at me, saying, "haram!", and he told me something that made my life at that time very difficult, "do not laugh in the *masjid*." I said, "I am sorry, I did not know, I am new here", he continued, "and when you laugh, do not show your teeth.". I was so confused, and because at that time, I was super sincere about making a change, I really want to flip my life now, I do not want nightlife and music anymore. I do not want that in my life anymore. But I have a little bit of a personality, like cracking jokes here and there, laughing a little but. But now, this guy told me that it is haram. And he said, "when you laugh, do not show your teeth.". So I went home to practise that. So I looked at the mirror, tried cracking a few jokes and laughed without showing my teeth. For hours, it did not work, I sounded like a monkey at the end. Anyway, ever since that, I refused to alter my emotions now, because Allah (s.w.t.) created these emotions for us to be felt. So do not allow anybody to tell us what emotions to feel.

A man came to Prophet (s.a.w.) asking for advice, so Prophet (s.a.w.) told him, "don't be angry". The man was not angry at that time. He was in fact very calm when he asked for the Prophet's (s.a.w.) advice. The Prophet did not see the man breaking glasses, throwing people, fighting and raging. All he asked for was an advice. He asked again, "what else can you give me?", "don't be angry", "what can you say?", "don't be angry". The Prophet mentioned it three times, why? Because he knew the man beforehand, he knew that this man had a temper. So that was the type of advice needed for that particular moment for this particular man.

A man said to the Prophet (ﷺ) , "Advise me! "The Prophet (ﷺ) said, "Do not become angry and furious." The man asked (the same) again and again, and the Prophet (ﷺ) said in each case, "Do not become angry and furious."

(Ṣaḥiḥ al-Bukhari 6116)

But didn't the Prophet (s.a.w.) himself got angry? He did. And we have the description on how the Prophet (s.a.w.) got angry. When ʿUmar ibn al-Khaṭṭab (r.a.) Came with the scrolls from the *Tawrah*, he was very excited when he showed it to the Prophet, he said, "I saw your name in the *Tawrah* scroll, he opened it, and Prophet (s.a.w.) remained silent.

Abu Bakr as-Ṣiddiq (r.a.) noticed that the Prophet (s.a.w.) was a little bit angry, so he told 'Umar, "enough, can't you see the Prophet? Can't you see that he is angry, and doesn't want you to proceed with this?" The Prophet at that time was very angry, his face turned red, and a very thick vein appeared on his forehead.

> Jabir told how 'Umar b. al-Khattab brought God's messenger a copy of the Torah saying, "Messenger of God, this is a copy of the Torah." When he received no reply he began to read to the obvious displeasure of God's messenger, so Abu Bakr said, "Confound you, do you not see how God's messenger is looking?" So 'Umar looked at God's messenger's face and said, "I seek refuge in God from the anger of God and His messenger. We are satisfied with God as Lord, with Islam as religion, and with Muḥammad as Prophet." Then God's messenger said, "By Him in whose hand Muḥammad's soul is, were Moses to appear to you and you were to follow him and abandon me, you would err from the right way. Were he alive and came in touch with my prophetic mission he would follow me."
>
> (Mishkat al-Maṣabiḥ 194)

So this is the point, emotions are results of circumstances and situations that happen right in front of our eyes. How could we not get angry if somebody pushed us against our will? So do not let anyone alter our emotions. We are entitled to feel our own feelings. But what we are not entitled to, is the action that followed. That action has to be in line with what Allah (s.w.t.) and His prophet approved.

Part 2:

The Importance Of Actions In Islam

So we have learn something about doing things for the sake of Allah, which means doing something without expecting anything in return from any human being, rather you do it to expect the reward and benefits from Allah (s.w.t.). And when Allah rewards us, He rewards it in a manner that we can never imagine. So we are going to put that into practice, and we will use a topic entitled 'love'. Choose a person who is standing next to you, and tell them, "I love you for the sake of Allah (s.w.t.), and the person should reply according to the sunnah, which is, "may the One whom you loved me for His sake, love you as well.", and then give each other the warmest hug.

THE IMPORTANCE OF ACTIONS IN ISLAM

Even though the Prophet (s.a.w.) clearly stated that we would not attain *Jannah*, that we would not enter *Jannah* unless Allah showers us with His mercy—not by our good actions, but rather by the mercy of Allah (s.w.t.). But that does not mean that actions in Islam are not important, in fact, actions are the evidence that we are submissive to Allah (s.w.t.), the evidence that we obey Him (s.w.t.). But in the Qur'an, Allah has commanded us in many places to do certain actions. The Prophet (s.w.t.) throughout his life had commanded us to execute certain actions, so if we do not do them to the best of our ability, we are disobedient, which means we are not fulfilling the meaning of Islam that has been mentioned earlier. We are a muslim still, we said لَا إِلَـٰهَ إِلَّا اللهُ مُحَمَّـدٌ رَسُـولُ اللهِ, but our Islam is not sufficient enough to take us to where we want to be, and that is *Jannah*.

The Prophet (s.a.w.) in a very famous narration said, بُنِـيَ الإِسْـلَامُ عَلَـى خَمْـس, which translates to 'Islam has been established upon five pillars, which means Islam is one thing, and the pillars are another thing.

> "(The superstructure of) al-Islam is raised on five (pillars), i. e. Allah (alone) should be worshipped, and (all other gods) beside Him should be (categorically) denied. Establishment of prayer, the payment of Zakat, Pilgrimage to the House, and the fast of Ramadan (are the other obligatory acts besides the belief in the oneness of Allah and denial of all other gods)."

> (Sahih Muslim, 16b)

And that is where we always go wrong, we live all our lives within the pillars but we forget to establish the *deen*, we forget to build the completion—the complete house of

Islam. The more we strengthen the pillars, the stronger the house of Islam. The pillars of Islam are meant for us to live, with a very powerful faith completing the house of Islam.

Where is truthfulness?

Where is being good to neighbours?

Where is being good to parents?

Where is the insistency of not to backbite?

Where is the insistency to not break promise?

The Prophet (s.a.w.) actually made things very clear regarding breaking promises. He (s.a.w.) said those who break promises are in the category of hypocrites.

"The Prophet (ﷺ) said, "The signs of a hypocrite are three: Whenever he speaks he tells a lie; whenever he is entrusted he proves dishonest; whenever he promises he breaks his promise.""

(Ṣaḥih al-Bukhari, 2749)

Prophet (s.a.w.) stated to identify a hypocrite, look for these three signs;

1. حَدَّثَ كَذَبَ

When he speaks, he utter lies.

2. وَإِذَا اؤْتُمِنَ خَانَ

When he is entrusted with something, he betrays the trust.

3. وَإِذَا وَعَدَ أَخْلَفَ

If he promise, he breaks the promise.

That is Islam, *ihsan* is a part of Islam.

There is a story of a lady who used to sell milk, and her mom told her to mix the milk with water since 'Umar ibn al-Khaṭṭab (r.a.), but the lady replied, "'Umar ibn al-Khaṭṭab (r.a.) is not here, but Allah is." 'Umar ibn al-Khaṭṭab (r.a.) heard the conversation, and he was impressed, not because of her prayer, or fasting, or even her *zakat*, but just due to that quality. Her pillars are strong, it resulted in her honesty and her *ihsan* in serving people. If our pillars are not strong, it will result in all of these vices that we are experiencing now, it will make us take our religion very lightly—we will compromise a lot with our religion. However, we cannot live only within the pillars of Islam all our lives. Rather, we have to establish our *deen* with Allah (s.w.t.) by practising, by taking actions.

And that is why Allah (s.w.t.) said in surah al-'Asr:

وَٱلْعَصْرِ ۝ إِنَّ ٱلْإِنسَـٰنَ لَفِى خُسْرٍ ۝ إِلَّا ٱلَّذِينَ ءَامَنُواْ وَعَمِلُواْ ٱلصَّـٰلِحَـٰتِ وَتَوَاصَوْاْ بِٱلْحَقِّ وَتَوَاصَوْاْ بِٱلصَّبْرِ ۝

"By the passage of time!, Surely humanity is in grave loss, except those who have faith, do good, and urge each other to the truth, and urge each other to perseverance."

(surah al-ʿAsr, 103:1-3)

Allah said, "by default we are all doomed.", we will never be saved by our own actions. "Except those who develop faith in Allah (s.w.t.), and execute righteous,". So the actions that we are referring to are good actions, rather than evil actions. Those evil actions must be fought against by all of us. We have the inclinations to do haram. Allah said in the Qur'an:

...إِنَّ ٱلنَّفْسَ لَأَمَّارَةٌ بِٱلسُّوٓءِ... ۝

"...for indeed the soul is ever inclined to evil..."

(surah Yusuf, 12:53)

Our own selves push us towards evil. We all have that tendency to do haram, but Allah (s.w.t.) also gave us the ability to control, to fight, and to resist it. He is giving us the criteria of successful people, if we want to be successful, we must have *iman*. Because once we have *iman* in our hearts, we would say our *shahadah*, أشــهد أن لا إلــه إلا الله وأشــهد أن محمــدا رســول الله, it is a way of us entering into Islam, which means *iman* comes first before Islam. And then the highest level of our belief is *ihsan*; to worship Allah as if He is right in front of us—as if we can see Him. But if we cannot, we are still fully aware that He sees us. He is always watching us, so how dare we do haram when we are alone, because Allah is there, watching us.

$$يَسْتَخْفُونَ مِنَ ٱلنَّاسِ وَلَا يَسْتَخْفُونَ مِنَ ٱللَّهِ وَهُوَ مَعَهُمْ... ﴿١٠٨﴾$$

"They try to hide their deception from people, but they can never hide it from Allah—in Whose presence…"

(surah an-Nisa', 4:108)

Allah (s.w.t.) complained about the situation of some

people who will conceal their sins from people, but they will not conceal it from Allah while He is with them. When we are behind closed doors, what are the chances for us not to go to any haram websites and watch these bad images? What are the chances?

There was this funny video surfacing the internet that some of us have watched before, a man withdrawing money from the ATM machine and someone was already waiting behind him, queuing. The man accidentally dropped his wallet, the person behind him saw the opportunity and decided to take the wallet and put it in his own pocket. After he stole the wallet, he looked up and saw a CCTV camera, he realised he was caught in the act. So he immediately took the wallet from his pocket and dropped it back on the floor. He tapped the man's shoulder and told the man that he dropped his wallet. The man thanked the 'thief' and continued his business. The 'thief' looked back at the camera and started apologising to the camera.

So when we are being watched, we tend to follow the rules. But if there are no 'cameras', we tend to break the rules. Unless there is constant awareness being raised about the danger of not being disciplined, people will do what they want to do. But once we apply these rules and policies, people tend to follow the rules.

Now, Allah is with us wherever we go, we are aware of this. So could we not develop *taqwa*—the God consciousness—that Allah is always watching over us? It will be difficult, it will not be easy. But when we start developing this quality; the stronger *it* gets, the better *we* get, in controlling and disciplining our lives. It is very difficult to maintain consistency. The answer is develop *taqwa*, study about what *taqwa* is, and the reward of *taqwa*.

The Prophet (s.a.w.) pointed at his heart and say, التَّقْـوَى هَاهُنَـا, "*taqwa* is in here."

"...Taqwa (piety) is right here [and he (s.a.w.) pointed to his chest three times]..."

(Hadith 35, 40 Hadith an-Nawawi)

Which means we have to work on our hearts, look at the act of worship that relies heavily on spirituality—reviving of the hearts, polishing our hearts. Look at the sins that we have always committed, going into the same cycle again and again. The Prophet (s.a.w.) said in a ḥadith:

"When the believer commits sin, a black spot appears on his heart. If he repents and gives up that sin and seeks forgiveness, his heart will be polished. But if (the sin) increases, (the black spot) increases. That is the Ran that Allah mentions in His Book: "Nay! But on their hearts is the Ran (covering of sins and evil deeds) which they used to earn." [83:14]

(Sunan ibn Majah 4244)

He (s.a.w.) said our heart develops a dark spot, and this black spot in our heart becomes rusty, it will make us not becoming receptive to the Qur'an, to the *du'a'*, to our *salah*. Our ears are always into music and movies, into fun activities related to the *dunya*. But when the Qur'an comes in, we cannot feel it.

We all have an interest in music. I was once like that as well, I used to be a musician, and I used to actually want music and Islam both ways. In fact, one of the funniest *du'a'* I had before I left music and come to Islam was, "Ya Allah, I love You so much, but I also like music a lot too, can I have it both ways please?" People kept telling me it is haram, but I was too attached to music, I could not leave it for a long time. So if I were to ask if music is halal or haram, I would answer it with, "I never ever remember a day in my life where music was a part of my life without actually not being interested in the *deen*." The *deen* would be a part-time thing for me. But once I left music, Qur'an fills that gap, it was difficult, but doable. Absolutely doable. So now, we all listen to music passively here and there, watching some entertainments, but intentionally going and enjoying it, that will affect our hearts and our religion; Islam.

So this is the criteria, action is a part of our lives as muslim. The Prophet (s.a.w.) mentioned in a ḥadith where he said:

$$إِنَّ اللَّهَ لاَ يَنْظُرُ إِلَى صُوَرِكُمْ وَأَمْوَالِكُمْ وَلَكِنْ يَنْظُرُ إِلَى قُلُوبِكُمْ وَأَعْمَالِكُمْ$$

Innallāha la yanẓuru ilā ṣuwarikum wa amwālikum walakin yanẓuru ilā qulubikum wa aʻmaalikum

"Verily Allah does not look to your faces and your wealth, but He looks to your heart and to your deeds."

(Saḥiḥ Muslim 2564c)

The intentions and the actions go hand in hand. We cannot have a good intention, but the action itself is not in accordance with the methodology of the Prophet (s.a.w.). If the intention is good and pure but the action is haram, both will be rejected by Allah (s.w.t.). If the action is good, but the intention is ruined, both will also be rejected by Allah (s.w.t.).

So our intention has to be good, and our actions must be in accordance with what Allah and His Messenger has told us.

«...يَا عِبَادِي! إِنَّمَا هِيَ أَعْمَالُكُمْ أُحْصِيهَا لَكُمْ، ثُمَّ أُوَفِّيكُمْ إِيَّاهَا؛ فَمَنْ وَجَدَ خَيْرًا فَلْيَحْمَدْ اللَّهَ، وَمَنْ وَجَدَ غَيْرَ ذَلِكَ فَلَا يَلُومَنَّ إِلَّا نَفْسَهُ»

"...O' My servants, it is but your deeds that I account for you, and then recompense you for. So he who finds good, let him praise Allah, and he who finds other than that, let him blame no one but himself."

(Saḥiḥ Muslim, 2577a)

Allah (s.w.t.) is singling out **only** the actions, in the previous ḥadith, Allah does not look into our appearances and wealth, but He looks into two things; our actions and our hearts. But in this particular ḥadith, Allah does not mention the heart, He only mentions our actions. He is keeping account for everything that we do—our actions. Allah (s.w.t.) will reward or punish us according to the actions we did. *"And whosoever on the day of Judgment found that his actions were so pleasing to Allah, then let him praise Allah, who guides him."* "*Alḥamdulillāh* who guided me to this, and had He

71

not guided me, I would have never been guided." So always give the credits to Allah who guided us to goodness.

"And whosoever found other than that—haram actions—let him blame no one but himself." So when it comes to bad actions, it is our own problems—our own choices.

We are all the results of our own choices, a result of our own habits that we have designed for ourselves. So when we introduce a habit to our brain, our brain does not recognise the harm or even the reward or benefit of that habit. The brain could only recognise the rush reward, if that action is rewardable, whether it is good or bad, halal or haram, there is a pleasure associated with it. If the brain recognises pleasure, the brain gets in control. It will start producing hormones; dopamine and endorphins, all these hormones to get us out of control. So we are not doing it out of consciousness anymore, rather it becomes a habit, an addiction. If the actions are too intense, and the reward is so great, it becomes an addictive behaviour.

World Health Organisation actually listed gaming as a mental disease; addiction. There are some parts of the world where someone died on their computer while playing games. Some even stopped eating, stopped using the toilet, just so that they can have more time in front of the computer to play. So be careful, if we give our brain too much of these activities, depending on the intensity of the games, we might even reach to that extreme level of addiction. May Allah protect us all.

CHAPTER 3:
THE SUCCESSFUL BELIEVERS

Allah (s.w.t.) begins surah al-Mu'minun with a very interesting verse:

$$\text{قَدْ أَفْلَحَ ٱلْمُؤْمِنُونَ}\ ①$$

"Successful indeed are the believers:"

(surah al-Mu'minun, 23:1)

The word قَدْ in arabic when it preceded anything in the past tense or in the future tense, it indicates **certainty**. This is exactly what is going to happen. There is no way this is not going to work. قَدْ أَفْلَحَ ٱلْمُؤْمِنُونَ, "indeed those successful believers are,"; those who does the following items or the following actions are the successful believers. So if we stick to those actions, we will be successful, according to this surah.

Now interestingly, when we read the surah, we will see that after every act of worship, comes an act of discipline or manners. Here is an example from the same surah:

$$\text{ٱلَّذِينَ هُمْ فِى صَلَاتِهِمْ خَٰشِعُونَ}\ ②$$

"those who humble themselves in prayer;"

(surah al-Mu'minun, 23:2)

The first criteria of those successful believers are those who when they pray, they concentrate. So TV is off, cooking is off. Everything we do worldly should come to oppose, because this is *ṣalah*. Many people ask how to develop focus and *khusyuʿ* in *ṣalah*, and this is how we should do it: When we establish the emergency state once *ṣalah* time is announced, leave everything in our hand. *Khusyuʿ* starts with *wuḍuʿ* by the way. When we walk to take our *wuḍuʿ*, we have that mental preparation that every part of our body that we wash, we are actually washing away our sins before coming to the prayer rug to pray. And the ayah after that:

"those who avoid idle talk;"

(surah al-Mu'minun, 23:3)

And those who turn away from ill talk or from unnecessary conversation—backbiting, lying, gossiping. And then the next verse proceeds with:

وَٱلَّذِينَ هُمْ لِلزَّكَوٰةِ فَعِلُونَ ٤

"those who pay alms-tax;"

(surah al-Mu'minun, 23:4)

And those who pays for their prescribed charities; *zakah*.

وَٱلَّذِينَ هُمْ لِفُرُوجِهِمْ حَـٰفِظُونَ ٥

"those who guard their chastity;"

(surah al-Mu'minun, 23:5)

And those who protect their private parts—those who keep themselves chaste. Those who when boys come and tell them, "I love you", they do not jump and say it back, instead they say, "well, go visit my father." Do not leave a long trace of conversation with a non-halal person because the end result will be haram.

But look at the order:

1. *Ṣalah*—prayers

    • They who are during their prayer humbly submissive.

2.   Avoiding ill speech

   • And they who turn away from ill speech.

3.   *Zakah*—obligatory charity

   • And they who are observant of *zakah*.

4.   Guarding the modesty

   • And they who guard their private parts.

Allah (s.w.t.) is talking about one act of worship followed by a manner, an ethic—something to establish in terms of dealing with one another. What we can do in our free time is: read surah al-Mu'minun and list down all the acts of worship on one line, and all acts of manners on another line. Then we can see that our beautiful religion is not only about the five pillars.

There was a story of the Prophet Muḥammad (s.a.w.) that his companion narrated on a lady who used to pray a lot, who used to give a lot of charity, and used to fast a lot, optionally. But she harmed her neighbours with her tongue. The Prophet (s.a.w.) did not indicate what sort of harm that this lady did with her tongue. She could be backbiting her neighbours, she could gossip a lot.

Abu Hurayra said,

"The Prophet, may Allah bless him and grant him peace, was asked, 'Messenger of Allah! A certain woman prays in the night, fasts in the day, acts and gives sadaqa, but injures her neighbours with her tongue.' The Messenger of Allah, may Allah bless him and grant him peace, said, 'There is no good in her. She is one of the people of the Fire.' They said, 'Another woman prays the prescribed prayers and gives bits of curd as sadaqa and does not injure anyone.' The Messenger of Allah, may Allah bless him and grant him peace, said, 'She is one of the people of the Garden.'"

(Al-Adab Al-Mufrad 119)

Backbiting according to the Prophet (s.a.w.) is to mention about someone else in their absence something that if they heard it, it will hurt them even if it is true. If it is untrue, if it is a lie, then it is called slandering (*buhtan*).

"It is reported by Qays that Amr bin al-Aas (ra) was going somewhere with his friends. They saw a dead mule whose belly had swollen up. Amr (ra) said, 'By Allah, it is better for one to eat to his full from this (dead mule) than to eat the flesh of a Muslim' (He meant to say that to backbite anyone is worse than eating the meat of a dead animal)."

(Al-Adab Al-Mufrad 736)

Gossiping however is different from backbiting. Gossiping is when we hear a story from a group of people of someone else, and we spread it to the particular person. We created a war between this person and that group of people.

»لا يدخل الجنة نمام«

"The Messenger of Allah (ﷺ) said, 'The person who goes about with calumnies (gossiping) will never enter *Jannah.*'"

(Riyad as-Salihin 1536)

And people asked, "Excuse me, what about the pillars of Islam?" Well, they are only pillars, they are not the whole house of Islam. Which is why the more we build, the more we strengthen the pillars, the more we perfected our *salah* and *zakah* and so on, the stronger the house will become. So we will have more resistance to say no to gossipers and backbiters. Even if they are our family members or our loved ones.

Here is another ḥadith to strengthen our pillars:

«...مَنْ كَانَ يُؤْمِنُ بِاللَّهِ وَالْيَوْمِ الآخِرِ...»

"...Whoever believes in Allah and the Last Day should talk about what is good or keep quiet,..."

(Ṣaḥīh al-Bukhari 6475)

This is Islam, our faith. It is not just about the *salah* in the *masjid*, it is not only about Ramaḍan, it is way broader than that.

CHAPTER 4:
ALLAH'S REVELATIONS

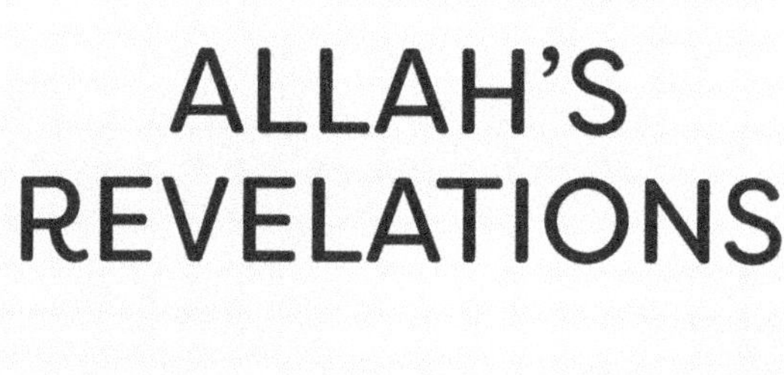

When we look at the first revelations, the first ayah in the Qur"an:

$$\text{اقْرَأْ بِاسْمِ رَبِّكَ الَّذِى خَلَقَ ﴿١﴾}$$

"Read, O Prophet, in the Name of your Lord Who created—"

(surah al-'Alaq, 96:1)

Is reading a verb or a noun? It is a verb, an action. But the man who received the revelations could not read, he never learned how to read before. He could not even recognise his own name. So what does that tell us, my brothers and sisters? It tells us that when Allah (s.w.t.) obliges us to do something, He requires us to find the way to execute it. Allah will not send us a catalogue on how to read, He asked us to exert an effort to come up with a solution, on how to read. So Allah's (s.w.t.) job is to command us, and our job is to find out how to execute the command.

Prophet (s.a.w.) kept on saying "I do not know how to read", and Jibril kept on saying, "اِقْرَأْ" (read). Did Allah not know that the Prophet (s.a.w.) could not read? Of course He knew. Did Jibril not know as well? Of course he knew too. So why was the command repeated? So that Prophet (s.a.w.) figured out a way on how to convey that message of reading, how to convey of sticking to the Qur'an. And *Alḥamdulillāh*, he did it. He memorised the word and started chanting them again and again.

So our job is to find a way, a solution on how to execute Allah's command. Do not give any excuses saying, "I cannot do this, I don't know how to do this." There are these people who always say 'cannot', they already made up their minds. Or saying "Allah made me this way," "I am angry because Allah created me like this, what can I do about it?" No, Allah never created us this way, because when we are angry, we look ugly, and Allah does not create anything ugly, ever. This is what we bring to ourselves. So if we develop a trait that is hated by Allah (s.w.t.), there are a lot of ways that we adjust.

The second surah that was revealed in the Qur'an is:

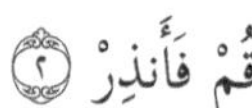

"Arise and warn all."

(surah al-Muddathir 74:1-2)

Allah's second revelation to Prophet (s.a.w.) is to stand up, leave the bed, and go convey the message. What is the message? To read, اِقْرَأْ. "In the name of Allah who created, tell them what you know."

84

The next revelation Allah sent to Prophet Muḥammad (s.a.w.) is:

$$قُمِ ٱلَّيْلَ إِلَّا قَلِيلًا ۝$$

"Stand all night in prayer except a little—"

(surah al-Muzammil, 73:2)

"Stand up now with whatever the Qur'an has been revealed to you, O' Muḥammad. Stand up all the night, except a little bit of it in prayers." How in the world was the Prophet (s.a.w.) able to stand up all night praying with only these three chapters in the Qur'an? If we read these three chapters now, it would only take us fifteen minutes. Again, the job of Allah is to reveal the command, and the job of the slaves is to execute it no matter what.

$$سَبِّحِ ٱسْمَ رَبِّكَ ٱلْأَعْلَى ۝$$

"Glorify the Name of your Lord, the Most High,"

(surah al-A'la, 87:1)

All these few chapters that were revealed are all action-oriented to tell us that our religion after the first revelation, is directing us towards working hard—*jihad* or *mujahadah*.

How many of us here really wants to pray *qiamullail* but are lazy? I am actually guilty of this too. I like watching soccer a lot, that is my weakness. I have two addictions in my life; one is coffee and second is football, do not judge me for this. So sometimes I watch the Premier League which sometimes starts at three in the morning. Me and my son would wake up just to watch it. But if he were asked to wake up for *tahajjud*, which would be around the same time, it would be difficult. Sometimes we are up at that time, but we do not pray still, correct? So in order to work around this, we have to fight ourselves, *mujahadah*. Keep doing it, just like caring for a small plant. If we keep watering it, it will slowly grow bigger, and Insha'Allāh maybe produce some fruits or vegetables. Actions is something very essential in Islam to keep our *iman* up par.

Part 3:

The Nullifiers Of Iman (Faith)

This is something very important because we would finally get to learn something that we probably has never know before. Something that could make us feel a bit miserable. I wish I did not make your life miserable by sharing this, but *wallahi*, what you will learn is going to make you realise that sometimes it is better to just to be quiet and ask people of knowledge, rather than just jump impulsively to be the centre of attention. Which could take us to area of *kufr*, may Allah protect us all. But just know that anything that is done unintentionally, Allah will not hold us accountable for. However, once we received the knowledge, now that we know, avoid to the best of our ability. And if we fall, and if we made the mistakes anyway, repent. So long as we are alive, repent. Because repentance will only come to an end the moment our soul leave our body. No more chances are given.

We may say لَآ إِلَـٰهَ إِلَّا اللّٰهُ مُحَمَّـدٌ رَسُـوْلُ اللّٰهِ (*Lai'lahaillallah Muhammadar Rasulullah*), and pray, do the *zakah*, all of these acts of worships, but we may say or do something that will nullify or cancel that faith. Just like when we make *wudu'* (ablution), how many of us when we make *wudu*, and went to the prayer rug, still wet, and something happened accidentally, like we unintentionally pass gas, we still have that *wudu'* water on our body, but something happened that nullify the *wudu*. Can we still pray with the *wudu'* water still on our body? No, we have to go renew, go take *wudu'* again.

The same thing goes with faith, it is in the heart, the mind, and the being of every individual. If we said or do something that nullify it, we have to renew our faith, we need to go back to our senses, ask Allah to forgive us, and renew our *shahadah*. Of course, it is not limited to what I have listed.

هُوَ ٱلَّذِى خَلَقَكُمْ فَمِنكُمْ كَافِرٌ وَمِنكُم مُّؤْمِنٌ ۚ وَٱللَّهُ بِمَا تَعْمَلُونَ بَصِيرٌ ۝

"He is the One Who created you, yet some of you are disbelievers while some are believers. And Allah is All-Seeing of what you do."

(surah at-Taghabun 64:2)

So first of all, some people said we cannot classify people as *kufr*. While that is true in some sense, according to the surah above, Allah (s.w.t.) already classified human beings as partially *kafir* and partially *mu'min*, that is why there is *Jannah* and *Jahannam*. Our job as a believer is to identify what could lead us to *Jannah*, and stick to it. Not only that, we have to also identify what could lead us to *Jahannam* so that we can avoid it. Just like the hadith:

89

» لَأَعْلَمَنَّ أَقْوَامًا مِنْ أُمَّتِي يَأْتُونَ يَوْمَ الْقِيَامَةِ بِحَسَنَاتٍ أَمْثَالِ جِبَالِ تِهَامَةَ بِيضًا فَيَجْعَلُهَا اللَّهُ عَزَّ وَجَلَّ هَبَاءً مَنْثُورًا « . قَالَ ثَوْبَانُ : يَا رَسُولَ اللَّهِ صِفْهُمْ لَنَا جَلِّهِمْ لَنَا أَنْ لاَ نَكُونَ مِنْهُمْ وَنَحْنُ لاَ نَعْلَمُ . قَالَ : » أَمَا إِنَّهُمْ إِخْوَانُكُمْ وَمِنْ جِلْدَتِكُمْ وَيَأْخُذُونَ مِنَ اللَّيْلِ كَمَا تَأْخُذُونَ وَلَكِنَّهُمْ أَقْوَامٌ إِذَا خَلَوْا بِمَحَارِمِ اللَّهِ انْتَهَكُوهَا « .

It was narrated from Thawban that the Prophet (ﷺ) said:

"I certainly know people of my nation who will come on the Day of Resurrection with good deeds like the mountains of Tihamah, but Allah will make them like scattered dust." Thawban said: "O Messenger of Allah, describe them to us and tell us more, so that we will not become of them unknowingly." He said: "They are your brothers and from your race, worshipping at night as you do, but they will be people who, when they are alone, transgress the sacred limits of Allah."

(Sunan ibn Majah 4245)

The Prophet (s.a.w.) he knows the people from our *ummah*—the Muslim *ummah*, come on the Day of Judgment with good deeds as big as the size of a mountain, but Allah will turn all of those good deeds into scattered dust, weightless, does not mean anything in the sight of Allah. The question now is why? People are doing good deeds, mountains of them. Why would Allah reject that? And Thawban (r.a.), one of the companions asked the Prophet to describe these people. Why does he care? Why would we care about the description of the bad people, the sinners? Because we want to avoid what they did, so that we do not end up in the same misery. And that is one of the mistakes that we always fall into; repeating the cycle of the people who have gone before us. We just keep on doing the same miserable things because of our culture, and keep on doing the haram all the time.

I was talking briefly to some people and came to know that many people are unable to get married because of the *mahar*. People make the halal super difficult, and the haram are available for free. Then, what are we expecting? Although the Prophet (s.a.w.) said, رَبِّـي يَسِّـرْ وَلاَ تُعَسِّـرْ, "Oh Allah, make this task easy and do not make it difficult." وَبَشِّـرَا وَلَا تُنَفِّـرَا, "and give good news to people before you struck them with bad news". وَتَطَاوَعَـا وَلَا تَخْتَلِفَـا, "always cooperate, always make things easy for the people, and do not get into conflicts unnecessarily with each other for little trivial matters."

وَعَـن ابنِ أَبِـي بُرْدَةَ قَالَ: بَعَـثَ النَّبِيُّ صَلَّى اللَّهُ عَلَيْـهِ وَسَـلَّمَ جَـدَّهُ أَبَـا مُوسَـى وَمُعَـاذًا إِلَـى الْيَمَـنِ فَقَـالَ: «يَسِّـرَا وَلَا تُعَسِّـرَا وَبَشِّـرَا وَلَا تُنَفِّـرَا وَتَطَاوَعَا وَلَا تَخْتَلِفَـا»

"Abu Burda told that when the Prophet sent his grandfather Abu Musa and Mu'adh to the Yemen he said,

'Make things easy and do not make them difficult; gladden and do not scare; comply with one another and do not disagree.'"

(Mishkat al-Masabih 3724)

All these things drag us away from our purpose, may Allah protect us all. But this ḥadith is very dangerous, because the people in subject here are not just Muslims, they are some of the elite Muslims. How did I know this? According to the previous ḥadith, Thawban (r.a.) asked Prophet Muḥammad (s.a.w.) to describe to us all, and he (s.a.w.) replied with, أَمَـا إِنَّهُـمْ إِخْوَانُكُمْ "indeed, they are your brothers and sisters", وَمِنْ جِلْدَتِكُمْ, "and they have the same inclinations like you", they are human beings, they have the same nature like you all, وَيَأْخُذُونَ مِنَ اللَّيْلِ كَمَا تَأْخُذُونَ, this is the extra quality of these people, "and the pray late at night just like you do", just like the companions who were asking the question. So they are not ordinary muslims, they are extraordinary, they leave their bed late at night to pray *tahajjud* for the sake of Allah (s.w.t.). So what is their problem then? What makes their actions go to ruin? وَلَكِنَّهُمْ أَقْوَامٌ إِذَا خَلَوْا بِمَحَارِمِ اللَّهِ انْتَهَكُوهَا, "but such people when they are behind closed doors, when they are alone and no one is watching them, they violate the rights of Allah."

So be careful, when we are alone, that is the criteria; if we want to measure our *taqwa*, we need to watch ourselves when we are alone. If we want to measure our *iman*, watch our actions when we are behind closed doors. This will tell us who we are as muslims, as a believer. But once we slip every time we are alone, we will develop a habit of once we are on the bed, on our phone, we are free to do whatever we want, we would probably fulfil the ḥadith mentioned above, may Allah protect us all.

Surah al-Kafirun is an example that when Allah (s.w.t.) told the muslims to convey the message, He said, "go and talk to the disbelievers." He addressed them in the Qur'an,

قُلْ يَـٰٓأَيُّهَا ٱلْكَـٰفِرُونَ, "O' you disbelievers", the word itself is not an insultive terms by the way. Some non-muslims, they hate the word *'kafir'* or infidel. I do not like the meaning of infidel as well, but *kafir* is a person who does not acknowledge Our truth. The Christians are *kafir* in what Allah (s.w.t.) said about Prophet Muḥammad (s.a.w.), they are *kafir* from that perspective. But we are also *kafir* in what they believe about Jesus—we deny that, we do not believe that Jesus is God or Son of God—we are *kafir* on that perspective. Basically, we are all *kafir* in some sense, when we deny certain aspects or beliefs.

Which is why Allah is very comfortable in addressing them in the Qur'an, "O' you, who have disbelieved or rejected My message." Because *kafir* here is a descriptive term, describing their condition. لَآ أَعْبُدُ مَا تَعْبُدُونَ, "I do not worship what you worship." So it is not really an insultive term.

But no one should ever classify a person as *kafir* unless he is a qualified scholar. This is very important because there is a ḥadith that goes:

"Allah's Messenger (ﷺ) said, 'If a man says to his brother, O Kafir (disbeliever)!' Then surely one of them is such (i.e., a Kafir).'"

(Ṣaḥiḥ al-Bukhari 6103)

"The Messenger of Allah (ﷺ) said, 'When a person calls his brother (in Islam) a disbeliever, one of them will certainly deserve the title. If the addressee is so as he has asserted, the disbelief of the man is confirmed, but if it is untrue, then it will revert to him.'"

(Riyaḍ as-Salihin 1732)

So if I call someone *kafir* without any knowledge, and I was wrong in my judgement about them, I will then be labelled by Allah as one, may Allah protect us all. But what if my judgement is right? If that person did and said something that qualify them as being a disbeliever, and a qualified scholar said that that person is a *kafir,* then on the Day Of Judgment, they will be labelled as such. The lesson is, never ever get into that area. This is for all of us, never get into that area of labelling each other as outsiders, because it might turn against us. So be careful.

CHAPTER 5:

WHAT NULLIFIES THE *IMAN*?

MOCKERY

Mockery or making unnecessary jokes about Allah and His Messenger, about the Qur'an. There was a group of people among the *sahabah* of the Prophet (s.a.w.) who were making fun of the Prophet, "is this the Messenger who will conquer Persia, as what people say? هَيْهَـاتَ هَيْهَـات (impossible, how impossible), he is dreaming." These people were making mockery of the Prophet (s.a.w.). So Allah revealed this *ayah*:

وَلَئِن سَأَلْتَهُمْ لَيَقُولُنَّ إِنَّمَا كُنَّا نَخُوضُ وَنَلْعَبُ قُلْ أَبِٱللَّهِ وَءَايَـٰتِهِۦ وَرَسُولِهِۦ كُنتُمْ تَسْتَهْزِءُونَ ۝ لَا تَعْتَذِرُواْ قَدْ كَفَرْتُم بَعْدَ إِيمَـٰنِكُمْ إِن نَّعْفُ عَن طَآئِفَةٍ مِّنكُمْ نُعَذِّبْ طَآئِفَةَ بِأَنَّهُمْ كَانُواْ مُجْرِمِينَ ۝

"If you question them, they will certainly say, 'We were only talking idly and joking around.' Say, 'Was it Allah, His revelations, and His Messenger that you ridiculed?' Make no excuses! You have lost faith after your belief. If We pardon a group of you, l We will punish others for their wickedness."

(surah at-Tawbah, 9:65-66)

Allah was questioning if it is Him or His Messenger, or His ayah that they were making a mockery of. And Allah continues with "do not even apologise". Those were the companions of the Prophet, people who were in the battlefield with the Prophet, those people were making a mockery about him being a simple and humble man. Allah said "do not even apologise, you have already disbelieved after you have acquired your iman." Just like the word قَدْ that I mentioned earlier, in the Qur'an, it indicates certainty, especially if it preceded or came before or appeared before a past tense. This is exactly what the Qur'an said, قَدْ كَفَرْتُـم, "you have already disbelieve" for certain. So this is one of the things that can nullify your faith.

In Egypt, I remember growing up, there are many words that are uncommon to the laypeople of Egypt. The dialect that we have developed in Egypt is not the Arabic of the Qur'an anymore. Some words in the deep Arabic of the Qur'an resemble other words that we used in an insultive manner sometimes, and are similar to the pronunciation. I remember many people using those words from the Qur'an, but actually referring to the haram aspect of the Egyptian word. That is very dangerous, we are playing with the Qur'an, playing with the words of Allah (s.w.t.). Avoid that. Prophet (s.a.w.) marriage to Ai'sha, "never ever say anything that you have no knowledge of". Never come to the area because this battle is guided with every breath of every minute of his life. This man is guided through all what he did and what he had established. If we do not understand the wisdom, we better ask. But never go beyond, or make our brain think that we are wiser than Allah, *Astagfirullāh*. Ask and be humble, but do not mock and make fun of anything related to Allah, the Qur'an, and Islam in general.

WHEN YOUR WORDS CONTRADICT YOUR ACTIONS

Contradicting is when we say *la i'laha illallah,* but we do not obey Allah (s.w.t.). There is a quote that most people often say nowadays, 'do not judge me', nobody is judging, we are only advising towards the halal and avoiding haram. They say they believe in Allah, but they do not follow Allah. What does that tell them?

Imagine if my wife is sick and she needs me to help her bring some water or medicines, but I am too busy doing the things I love that I neglect her, my own wife. Does that really mean that I love my wife? No. If our loved ones need us and we are there to help, then our actions will be the proof that what we said—that we love them—is true.

So when we say, *la i'laha illallah* but we do not pray, then what is the point? Be careful, because this will make us fall into the area of *kufr*.

« من قال لا إله إلا الله ، وكفر بما يعبد من دون الله، حرم ماله ودمه، وحسابه على الله تعالى»

"He who professes *La ilaha illallah* (There is no true god except Allah), and denies of everything which the people worship besides Allah, his property and blood become inviolable, and it is for Allah to call him to account".

(Riyaḍ as-Saliḥin 391)

So if we say *la i'laha illallah* and we disbelieve—we deny all other deities, then Allah (s.w.t.) will make Hellfire haram to burn us and everything that we have accumulated. Because we acted upon the meaning of *la i'laha illallah;* to deny any other way of life except that which Allah has brought to us.

Which is why the *shahadah* itself is divided into two parts; *la i'laha* and *illallah.* The first part means 'there is no God', so in order for us to acknowledge Allah, we have to deny all other deities, 'there is no God worthy of worship except Allah'. So it is negation of any deities except Allah. It is an affirmation that we only worship Allah (s.w.t.) and we are ready to obey Him.

A quick comparison between *illah* and *rabb*, when we read surah al-Fatiḥah we say:

$$\text{ٱلْحَمْدُ لِلَّهِ رَبِّ ٱلْعَٰلَمِينَ ۝}$$

"All praise is for Allah—Lord of all worlds,"

(surah al-Fatiḥah, 1:2)

And when we are making the testimony of our faith, we say, "*la i'laha illallah*". We do not say "*la i'laha rabbaallah*".

Rabb means owner, master, cherisher, sustainer, and maintainer of the entire universe. Even disbelievers, the Quraysh, they believe in *rabb*. They believe in Allah as the creator of the universe.

I'laha means worshipped, obeyed, to be followed. Which is why we use *i'laha* when we say "*la i'laha illallah*", none can be worshipped, obeyed, and followed except Allah (s.w.t.), none. If we look at *shaytan* and his acknowledgement, he said in surah Ṣad:

$$\text{قَالَ أَنَا۠ خَيْرٌ مِّنْهُ ۖ خَلَقْتَنِى مِن نَّارٍ وَخَلَقْتَهُۥ مِن طِينٍ ۝}$$

"He replied, 'I am better than he is: You created me from fire and him from clay.'"

(surah Ṣad, 38:76)

In reference to Prophet Adam (a.s.), *shaytan* said, 'You created me', so *shaytan* acknowledged that Allah is the creator. But when Allah commanded *shaytan* to prostrate to Adam, he refused. *Shaytan* believed Allah as *rabb*, but not as *i'laha*.

Many times we fall into the same thing, many times we preferred the *dunya*. So we need to be careful. Allah said in the Qur'an:

$$\text{وَلَئِن سَأَلْتَهُم مَّنْ خَلَقَ ٱلسَّمَٰوَٰتِ وَٱلْأَرْضَ وَسَخَّرَ ٱلشَّمْسَ وَٱلْقَمَرَ لَيَقُولُنَّ ٱللَّهُ ۖ فَأَنَّىٰ يُؤْفَكُونَ ۝}$$

"If you ask them 'O' Prophet who created the heavens and the earth and subjected the sun and the moon for your benefit', they will certainly say,

'Allah!' How can they then be deluded from the truth?"

(surah al-'Ankabut, 29:61)

So what was the problem with the Quraysh, the people of Makkah? If they believe that Allah is the creator of the heavens and the earth, then what was their problem? Because they worshipped other than Him. they worshipped 360 Gods along with Allah (s.w.t.) or beside Him. That is why they were considered *kafir musyrik*.

ASSISTING NON-MUSLIMS AGAINST MUSLIMS

To aid the disbelievers against our own brothers and sisters of faith. I will never forget when I was younger, way before I started practising Islam, I had a Pakistani brother, Ashraf, may Allah bless him. He lost a lot of his family members including his brother in the events in Palestine while he was in Egypt. One day he told me that the Egyptian government will open the gates for the Palestinians who have been injured to come into Egypt and seek some medical help and assistance there. I was very happy to go with him and experience the moments. We saw the police and troops coming in and preventing us from assisting our Palestinian brothers who were injured. I would never forget the person that I have seen whose hands were almost detached from his body, and we saw the gates being shut in front of our brothers and sisters in Palestine. Why? Because there was an agreement between Egypt and the Zionist. I do not want to get into politics much, but if we read and see the recent happenings to our brothers and sisters in Egypt, seeing how they were treated, we would be questioning ourselves, "are they (the Egyptians) really a Muslim?".

So assisting the non-Muslims against our own brothers and sisters is an area that can actually nullify our iman.

۞ يَـٰٓأَيُّهَا ٱلَّذِينَ ءَامَنُوا۟ لَا تَتَّخِذُوا۟ ٱلْيَهُودَ وَٱلنَّصَـٰرَىٰٓ أَوْلِيَآءَ ۘ بَعْضُهُمْ أَوْلِيَآءُ بَعْضٍ ۚ وَمَن يَتَوَلَّهُم مِّنكُمْ فَإِنَّهُۥ مِنْهُمْ ۗ إِنَّ ٱللَّهَ لَا يَهْدِى ٱلْقَوْمَ ٱلظَّـٰلِمِينَ ﴿٥١﴾

"O' believers! Take neither Jews nor Christians as guardians—they are guardians of each other. Whoever does so will be counted as one of them. Surely Allah does not guide the wrongdoing people."

(surah al-Ma'idah, 5:51)

KUFR; *ZINA* (ADULTERY) AND NEGLIGENCE IN *ṢALAH*

I put *zina* and negligence in *ṣalah* together because they fall into the same category as *kufr*. The Prophet (s.a.w.) said:

» لاَ يَزْنِي الزَّانِي حِينَ يَزْنِي وَهْوَ مُؤْمِنٌ، وَلاَ يَسْرِقُ حِينَ يَسْرِقُ وَهْوَ مُؤْمِنٌ، وَلاَ يَشْرَبُ حِينَ يَشْرَبُهَا وَهْوَ مُؤْمِنٌ، وَالتَّوْبَةُ مَعْرُوضَةٌ بَعْدُ «.

"The one who commits an illegal sexual intercourse is not a believer at the time of committing illegal sexual intercourse and a thief is not a believer at the time of committing theft and a drinker of alcoholic drink is not a believer at the time of drinking. Yet, (the gate of) repentance is open thereafter."

(Ṣaḥiḥ al-Bukhari 6810)

A person at the time of *zina* is not a believer, because this is not the action that a believer should perform. Just like how we strip off our shirt, that is how our *iman* will be stripped off our hearts.

Now the scholars debate on the meaning of *kufr* here,

105

the majority said these people are still a muslim, but their *iman* is incomplete. But some scholars actually stick to the literal meaning of the word that the Prophet (s.a.w.) said, that those who commit *zina* are a disbeliever.

So what are the chances of us to commit those actions, *na'udhubillah min zalik*, relying on the fact that we will still be muslims, according to that one opinion when there is the other opinion that stated that we are probably *kafir*? May Allah protect us all. Anything that leads us to *zina* should be avoided.

What are the things that could introduce us to *zina* without us realising it?

لعينان زِنَاهُمَا النَّظَرُ وَالْأُذُنَانِ زِنَاهُمَا الِاسْتِمَاعُ وَاللِّسَانُ زِنَاهُ الْكَلَامُ وَالْيَدُ زِنَاهَا الْبَطْشُ وَالرِّجْلُ زِنَاهَا الْخُطَا وَالْقَلْبُ يَهْوَى وَيَتَمَنَّى وَيُصَدِّقُ ذَلِكَ الْفَرْجُ وَيُكَذِّبُهُ

"The fornication of the eyes consists in looking, of the ears in hearing, of the tongue in speech, of the hand in violence, and of the foot in walking. The heart lusts and wishes, and the private parts accord with that or reject it."

(Mishkat al-Maṣabiḥ 86)

The Prophet (s.a.w.) said our eyes commit *zina*; the *zina* of the eyes is to stare in lustful activities and lustful imagery. Those who watch and are addicted to these lustful images, *wal iyadzubillah*, they are committing *zina* of the eyes. Because we are looking at the pictures and the images of people not wearing anything and acting upon these sexual activities, and seeking pleasure through their performances, and that is an absolute haram act, that is *zina*. Our brain will keep on getting overstimulated by these images to a point where we will start getting bored with the images and needing the real thing. So most people who are addicted to these images fall into *zina*. Even our ears commit *zina*, by hearing anything haram. Our tongue, speaking about anything haram, our hands and feet. All these things lead us to *zina*, the actual act.

These following items are a gateway to *zina*—the tenth most serious sin in Islam—which we have observed before.

1. Social media.

When we are on social media, we need to avoid all those images, the pages, the accounts. Especially now with the algorithm, where if we actually visited any of

those pages or accounts, sometimes an advertisement related to it pops up. And that will feed our brain with the images and lead us to *zina*.

2. Chatting.

Of course chatting unnecessarily with the opposite gender, getting used to each other's company. I have also seen this among people of *da'wah*, people of the Islamic upbringing. Because they did not create limits between themselves and the opposite gender, hence, *shayṭan* overcame them. May Allah protect us all.

3. Pornography.

One of the leading causes of not only *zina*, but divorces, mental health, and our physical brain, leading to lack of motivation, lack of memory, and lack of decision making. In fact, decision making impairment can be caused by watching these images repeatedly. As I mentioned earlier, once our brain gets addicted to highly intense products, whether it is a substance or an image, people will tend to act out of these fantasies.

There is a story of how these images can impact our brain, an Indian movie that I used to watch when I was younger, a Bollywood movie. The imagination of this movie is very intense, I remembered there was this British army coming into the village, destroying everything and killing everybody. A man in charge of saving this village decided to mount his wife and his newly born baby on a horse so that they could leave the village while he fought with the armies. He thought he would not recognised his baby once he grow up later in the future, so he decided to carve his name on his child's chest with a knife. Out of all options he could make, he decided to use a sharp knife. As he was carving his name, baby writhing in pain, the music played in the background is always a sad music which make people cry as well. Because this movie would not happen in real life, the imaginary made me want to act out the scene. I was the main character, and because I was so young back then, I did not know any better, I hurt myself trying to act out the scene, I carved my own name. When I went to sleep, I took off my shirt because the wound was too itchy. I woke up to my dad laughing at me, so I lied and told him my sister did it.

My point is, these imaginations of the images can spoil our brain and make us believe that they are real. So when it comes to pornography, it can be even harder. There is a name to it, 'supernormal stimulus', it makes us feel that what we have observed and watched, we can actually do it in real life situations. When we try to apply it with our spouse, things go wrong, we are not satisfied with it because we could not perform the same way as how that industry demonstrates it.

»العهـد الـذي بيننـا وبينهـم الصـلاة، فمـن تركهـا فقـد كفـر«

"That which differentiates us from the disbelievers and hypocrites is our performance of salat. He who abandons it, becomes a disbeliever."

(Riyaḍ as-Saliḥin 1079)

Again the scholars debated on the meaning of *kufr* here, but what are the chances? Are we willing to give a chance to ourselves to fall into that area? So leave it off completely. All of these things that can nullify our faith, our *iman*. May Allah (s.w.t.) protect us all. **And whatever we have in this *dunya*, nothing that we work for, nothing that we run after will overweigh *iman*.** If we lost iman, we lost everything. If we maintain *iman*, but we lost everything in this *dunya*, then it is worth it.

وَٱلْءَاخِرَةُ خَيْرٌ وَأَبْقَىٰٓ ۝

"even though the Hereafter is far better and more lasting."

(surah al-A'la, 87:17)

The Prophet (s.a.w.) mentioned that this is equal to a wing of a mosquito to Allah (s.w.t.), but we run after it as if it is everything.

لَوْ كَانَتِ الدُّنْيَا تَعْدِلُ عِنْدَ اللَّهِ جَنَاحَ بَعُوضَةٍ,...

"If the world to Allah was equal to a mosquito's wing,..."

(Jami' at-Tirmidhi 2320)

TO DISLIKE THE RULES OF ALLAH (S.W.T.)

This is what I mentioned regarding polygamy. If you dislike it in the sense of rejecting it, ذَٰلِكَ بِأَنَّهُمْ كَرِهُوا, Allah (s.w.t.) classify those people as disbelievers because they have disliked the rules of Allah that have been revealed.

وَٱلَّذِينَ كَفَرُواْ فَتَعْسًا لَّهُمْ وَأَضَلَّ أَعْمَـٰلَهُمْ ۝ ذَٰلِكَ بِأَنَّهُمْ كَرِهُواْ مَآ أَنزَلَ ٱللَّهُ فَأَحْبَطَ أَعْمَـٰلَهُمْ ۝

"As for the disbelievers, may they be doomed and may He render their deeds void. That is because they detest what Allah has revealed, so He has rendered their deeds void."

(surah Muḥammad, 47:8-9)

We may dislike, we may feel that it is awkward, it is weird, it is something that we cannot do or apply in our lives. We can ask and inquire but never develop any hate for the religion because of a rule that Allah (s.w.t.) revealed for the benefits of some people. Of course, sometimes not all the rules will be applied to everyone. So if we rejected the rule and we felt that the rule is not applicable to us, just know that there are many other people that can benefit from those rule.

IMITATING DISBELIEVERS

مَنْ تَشَبَّهَ بِقَوْمٍ فَهُوَ مِنْهُمْ

"He who copies any people is one of them."

(Mishkat al-Maṣabih 4347)

The Prophet (s.a.w.) said if we ever imitate a group of people, we will either be with them in *Jannah*, or in *Jahannam*.

"The Prophet (ﷺ) said, 'You will follow the ways of those nations who were before you, span by span and cubit by cubit (i.e., inch by inch) so much so that even if they entered a hole of a mastigure, you would follow them.' We said, 'O' Allah's Messenger (ﷺ)! (Do you mean) the Jews and the Christians?' He said, 'Whom else?'"

(Ṣaḥih al-Bukhari 7320)

The prophet said his *ummah* will follow them to an extent if they went through a lizard hole, they will still follow them. That was the conditions of the believers at one point, so let us not be like them. He asks us to be different from those who associate partners with Allah (s.w.t.), which is why *salatul jum'a* is on Friday instead of Saturday and Sunday.

Part 4:

Returning to Allah (S.w.t.)

CHAPTER 6: SINNING

BEFORE THE SIN

How to deal with the situation before the sin. We all err—we all commit mistakes, we all fall into errors. But what can we do before the sin? We have to ask ourselves what actually led us to sinning?

I am sure that some of us realised that we are all addicted to gadgets, our phones. All of us are constantly stuck to our phones. But how many of us found out that being on the phone too much leads to haram activities?

Once we realise this, we have to make a plan. We now know that our gadgets are the source of our sins, so what can we do before that? We have to change our environment. When our Prophet (s.a.w.) migrated from Makkah to Madina, the first he did was building a masjid. He refused to go to any home, because if he went to any home that people invited him to, he would probably be too relaxed, sleeping, and enjoying the fun and the generosity of the people, and did not do the job that is required of him. Once the *masjid* was built, it became the hub of the muslims for prayers, meetings, and classes.

So when our environment is conducive to *iman*-driven activities, nothing can shake us. Imagine if we are in front of the Ka'bah, will we be able to do the haram stuff? Most likely not, because the environment is too holy for us to commit sin. So what we can do is, look at our home, our room, our surroundings and make some modifications, so that even if we want to do the haram, our new environment prevents us from doing so. Make a small station outside of the bedroom to leave any gadgets from entering the room, make this a rule. To never bring any gadgets inside the bedroom, and to not use it after a certain period of time.

Environments breed actions. Once we design a specific environment, an action is born, naturally. If the environment is toxic, then every action within the environment will also be toxic.

DURING THE SIN

Now that we have recognised the loop of the sin, the same cycle is going to happen. Take Prophet Yusuf (a.s.) when he was seduced by the lady, when the lady asked him to do zina. She shut the doors, locked every window, and put guards outside to prevent people from coming in. She said to Prophet Yusuf (a.s.) هَيْتَ لَكَ, 'come here'. Prophet Yusuf said when we are about to fall, the first thing we should do is call upon Allah (s.w.t.). Call upon Him, run to Him. No one will save us at that time except Allah (s.w.t.).

وَرَٰوَدَتْهُ ٱلَّتِى هُوَ فِى بَيْتِهَا عَن نَّفْسِهِۦ وَغَلَّقَتِ ٱلْأَبْوَٰبَ وَقَالَتْ هَيْتَ لَكَ ۚ قَالَ مَعَاذَ ٱللَّهِ ۖ إِنَّهُۥ رَبِّىٓ أَحْسَنَ مَثْوَاىَ ۖ إِنَّهُۥ لَا يُفْلِحُ ٱلظَّٰلِمُونَ ۝

"And the lady, in whose house he lived, tried to seduce him. She locked the doors firmly and said, 'Come to me!' He replied, 'Allah is my refuge! It is not right to betray my master, who has taken good care of me. Indeed, the wrongdoers never succeed.'"

(surah Yusuf, 12:23)

He did other things well, he tried to run away when she tore his shirt off, he was resisting. Run away as far as we can from the place where sin is about to happen. Try talking to someone to distract from doing something haram, because once we talk about something different, our brain will divert our attention to that new thing.

AFTER THE SIN

Again, because we are all human beings, we err. We will commit mistakes. So if we commit a mistake, the first thing we should do is despair not from the mercy of Allah (s.w.t.).

قُلْ يَـٰعِبَادِىَ ٱلَّذِينَ أَسْرَفُوا۟ عَلَىٰٓ أَنفُسِهِمْ لَا تَقْنَطُوا۟ مِن رَّحْمَةِ ٱللَّهِ ۚ إِنَّ ٱللَّهَ يَغْفِرُ ٱلذُّنُوبَ جَمِيعًا ۚ ... ۝

"Say, O' Prophet, that Allah says, 'O My servants who have exceeded the limits against their souls! Do not lose hope in Allah's mercy, for Allah certainly forgives all sins.'"

(surah az-Zumar, 39:53)

Allah said to tell His servants who have wronged themselves day and night, sinning here and there. Tell them despair not to the mercy of Allah, because He forgives all sins. So no matter what we did, Allah will forgive so long as we constantly repent. We all sin, as what the Prophet (s.a.w.) said:

كُلُّ بَنِي آدَمَ خَطَّاءٌ وَخَيْرُ الْخَطَّائِينَ التَّوَّابُونَ

"Every son of Adam commits sin, and the best of those who commit sin are those who repent."

(Sunan ibn Majah 4251)

اتَّقِ اللَّهَ حَيْثُمَا كُنْتَ وَأَتْبِعِ السَّيِّئَةَ الْحَسَنَةَ تَمْحُهَا

وَخَالِقِ النَّاسَ بِخُلُقٍ حَسَنٍ

"Have taqwa of Allah wherever you are, and follow an evil deed with a good one to wipe it out, and treat the people with good behaviour"

(Jami' at-Tirmidhi 1987)

So despair not, follow the sin with good deeds, good deeds will wipe out the bad ones, so do not just sit in the corner and cry over your conditions. If we have sin, we repent again and again.

THE WAY FORWARD

Now that we have learned from our mistakes, we have to re-design our environment as mentioned earlier, then establish a solid system; the do's and don'ts in our lives, friends to boycott and friends to stay close to. Because friends have a lot of influence in our lives, the person who we thought was our best friend, but then they turn around and stab us in the back. I am pretty sure that we have experienced that at least once in our lives.

Implement what we have promised ourselves to implement. Once we have said, "I am going to start doing this", stick to it, and make it public.

إِنَّ ٱلَّذِينَ قَالُوا۟ رَبُّنَا ٱللَّهُ ثُمَّ ٱسْتَقَـٰمُوا۟ تَتَنَـزَّلُ عَلَيْهِـمُ ٱلْمَلَـٰٓئِكَةُ أَلَّا تَخَافُوا۟ وَلَا تَحْزَنُوا۟ وَأَبْشِـرُوا۟ بِٱلْجَنَّةِ ٱلَّتِى كُنتُمْ تُوعَدُونَ ﴿٣٠﴾

"Surely those who say, 'Our Lord is Allah,' and then remain steadfast, the angels descend upon them, saying, 'Do not fear, nor grieve. Rather, rejoice in the good news of Paradise, which you have been promised.'"

(surah al-Fussilat, 41:30)

Part 5:

Being Consistent

CHAPTER 7:

HOW TO STICK TO YOUR PLAN

DU'A' (الدعاء)

Now that we want to stick to the system that we have talked about, being consistent. The first thing we should know is that we will never achieve anything without *du'a'*, which is what the Prophet said:

$$\text{الدُّعَاءُ مُخُّ الْعِبَادَةِ}$$

"The supplication is the essence of worship."

(Jami' at-Tirmidhi 3371)

So *du'a'* (supplication) to Allah is *'ibadah*. That is what the Prophet (s.a.w.) mentions. Which means if we do not do *du'a'*, we are not fulfilling our main purpose of this *dunya*. Allah said, "I created you to worship Me.", and Prophet (s.a.w.) said "*du'a'* is *'ibadah*", so if we do not do *du'a'*, then we are not fulfilling our *'ibadah*, so we are not fulfilling our purpose of existence.

So if we do not spend our time every day, yes, every day, raising up our hands, begging Allah to change our situations in our favour, hence, we are actually neglecting that part of our lives, of why we are created in the first place.

When we make *du'a'* asking Allah for steadfastness while

adhering to the requirements that He has been placed upon us, most likely Allah (s.w.t.) will answer our prayers and direct us in the right path, *Insha'Allāh*.

These are some of the examples of the *duʿā* in the Qur'an, if we read surah al-Fatiḥah alone, ask ourselves, "how did Allah (s.w.t.) tell us to recite al-Fatiḥah every day in every prayer and in every rakʿah, ٱهْدِنَا ٱلصِّرَٰطَ ٱلْمُسْتَقِيمَ, 'guide us to the straight path', then did Allah not guide us already for being a Muslim?"

"Guide us along the straight path"

(surah al-Fatiḥah, 1:6)

So why must we repeat the words again and again? Because ٱهْدِنَا (guide us) in that context does not necessarily mean to bring us to Islam. It means to keep us upon Islam. So when we constantly ask Allah for *hidayah*, we are not asking Him to bring us to Islam, we are already a Muslim, *Alḥamdulillāh*, we are asking Him to cause us to die as a Muslim.

رَبَّنَا لَا تُزِغْ قُلُوبَنَا بَعْدَ إِذْ هَدَيْتَنَا وَهَبْ لَنَا مِن لَّدُنكَ رَحْمَةً ۚ إِنَّكَ أَنتَ ٱلْوَهَّابُ ﴿٨﴾

"[They say,] 'Our Lord! Do not let our hearts deviate after you have guided us. Grant us Your mercy. You are indeed the Giver [of all bounties].'"

(surah al-Imran, 3:8)

SINCERE COMMITMENT (الالتزام)

When we worship Allah (s.w.t.), we have to worship with absolute sincere commitment, that this is our job as a slave of Allah. For example if the husband asks the wife to take off their hijab, say no. The Prophet (s.a.w.) commanded the women to follow their husband, so long as they follow Allah.

The Prophet (s.a.w.) said:

لَا طَاعَةَ لِمَخْلُوقٍ فِي مَعْصِيَةِ اللَّهِ عَزَّ وَجَلَّ

"There is no obedience to any created being if it involves disobedience to Allah, may He be glorified and exalted."

(Musnad Aḥmad 1095)

So do not let people twist the knowledge of Allah (s.w.t.) and make us believe in something different.

وَلَوْ أَنَّا كَتَبْنَا عَلَيْهِمْ أَنِ اقْتُلُوٓا أَنفُسَكُمْ أَوِ اخْرُجُوا مِن دِيَـٰرِكُم مَّا فَعَلُوهُ إِلَّا قَلِيلٌ مِّنْهُمْ ۖ وَلَوْ أَنَّهُمْ فَعَلُوا مَا يُوعَظُونَ بِهِۦ لَكَانَ خَيْرًا لَّهُمْ وَأَشَدَّ تَثْبِيتًا ۝

"If We had commanded them to sacrifice themselves or abandon their homes, none would have obeyed except for a few. Had they done what they were advised to do, it would have certainly been far better for them and more reassuring,"

(surah an-Nisa', 4:66)

Imagine if Allah said that if we believe He is our creator, our sustainer, that He is the One that gave us everything, He will put us into a test, by telling us to 'kill yourselves', will we do it? Will we obey Him? This is just an example from Allah, He is not going to order us to kill ourselves, He will ask us to do certain things that will guarantee us a place in *Jannah*.

So sincere commitment means to follow Allah, to obey Him in whatever He commands us to do, *Insha'Allāh*.

KNOWLEDGE (العلم)

Every single person that read this book is now responsible for this knowledge. This knowledge becomes a property to those who are currently reading this. Every single knowledge that we have learned today becomes our property, our responsibility, no excuses. This part of the property if it is not fulfilled, if we do not apply that knowledge, we would be responsible for it. Imam al-Ghazali said:

$$العلم بلا عمل جنون والعمل بغير علم لا يكون$$

"Knowledge without action is madness, and actions with no knowledge do not exist."

If we have the knowledge but do not act upon it, we are insane. And actions with no knowledge do not exist, we cannot act randomly without certain knowledge. I remember asking a friend of mine to drive his car but I do not know how to drive, when he asked, I lied. Because we Egyptians and Arabians in general do not know how to say "I don't know". So when I get the car, I looked at the gear and I moved it randomly, and it worked, it moved forward. But then I realised, that was not my doing, I was actually on a high hill. The next minute, I was hugging a tree. I did not have any knowledge of driving, which was why I crashed the car. So if we do not have the right knowledge, it will cause disasters. But once we receive a certain know;edge, we act upon it.

People always say, 'knowledge is power', I do not believe that, however, I believe in this following statement and I hope people can redefine that previous knowledge. I believe in 'implementation of knowledge is power'. Yes, we know a lot of things, but that did not give us any power because we do not apply them. So applying the knowledge will cause that power.

The knowledge of the religion of Allah (s.w.t.) is unrivalled in its efficacy. Once we have gained an understanding of the rules and commands that are outlined in the Qur'an and through the teachings of our beloved Prophet (s.a.w.), it will be exceedingly difficult for us to stray from the path that leads to *Jannah*.

Allah (s.w.t.) referred to the condition of those who lacked adequate knowledge of the *deen* as blind, which usually means 'misguided'.

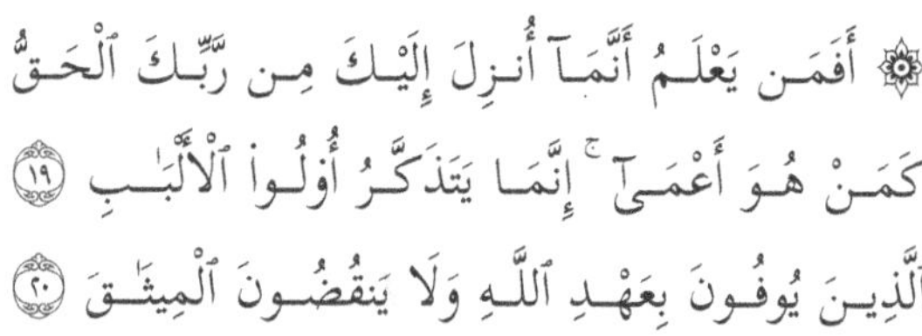

"Can the one who knows that your Lord's revelation to you [O Prophet] is the truth be like the one who is blind? None will be mindful [of this] except people of reason. [They are] those who honour Allah's covenant, never breaking the pledge;"

(surah ar-Ra'd, 13:19-20)

The knowledge of this beautiful دِين is a light that will serve us as we navigate in a world where many people's ideas, beliefs, desires, and aspirations are flat-out contradictions with what Allah (s.w.t.) had revealed. Allah said:

أَوَمَن كَانَ مَيْتًا فَأَحْيَيْنَٰهُ وَجَعَلْنَا لَهُۥ نُورًا يَمْشِى بِهِۦ فِى ٱلنَّاسِ كَمَن مَّثَلُهُۥ فِى ٱلظُّلُمَٰتِ لَيْسَ بِخَارِجٍ مِّنْهَا ۚ كَذَٰلِكَ زُيِّنَ لِلْكَٰفِرِينَ مَا كَانُوا۟ يَعْمَلُونَ ﴿١٢٢﴾

"Can those who had been dead, to whom We gave life and a light with which they can walk among people, be compared to those in complete darkness from which they can never emerge? That is how the misdeeds of the disbelievers have been made appealing to them."

(surah al-An'am, 6:122)

"There will come to the people years of treachery, when the liar will be regarded as honest, and the honest man will be regarded as a liar; the traitor will be regarded as faithful, and the faithful man will be regarded as a traitor; and the Ruwaibidah will decide matters.' It was said: 'Who are the Ruwaibidah?' He said: 'Vile and base men who control the affairs of the people.'"

(Sunan ibn Majah 4036)

RIGHTEOUS COMPANY (الصحبة الصالحة)

The righteous company is one of the key points that Allah spoke in the Qur'an in surah al-Kahf, if we have been reading it every Friday as what Prophet (s.a.w.) advised us to, we noticed that there is an *ayah* where Allah (s.w.t.) is telling us:

$$ \text{وَٱصْبِرْ نَفْسَكَ مَعَ ٱلَّذِينَ يَدْعُونَ رَبَّهُم بِٱلْغَدَوٰةِ وَٱلْعَشِيِّ ... ﴿٢٨﴾} $$

"And patiently stick with those who call upon their Lord morning and evening,..."

(surah al-Kahf, 18:28)

That should be the focus when choosing a friend. Choose a friend who is attached to Allah (s.w.t.), who when we meet, we would always remember Allah. Those people who are dedicated in worshipping Allah day and night, be with them. Once we are in those circles, we will become like them all.

$$ \text{يَٰٓأَيُّهَا ٱلَّذِينَ ءَامَنُوا۟ ٱتَّقُوا۟ ٱللَّهَ وَكُونُوا۟ مَعَ ٱلصَّٰدِقِينَ ﴿١١٩﴾} $$

"O' believers! Be mindful of Allah and be with the truthful."

(surah at-Tawbah, 9:119)

When we are always with the truthful, we will most likely become a truthful person ourselves. The people we spend the most time with has an effect on us, for better or for worse. Prophet (s.a.w.) said, a man or a woman is always inclined to follow the religion of his or her friends, so watch out who our friends are.

> "The Prophet (ﷺ) said: A man follows the religion of his friend; so each one should consider whom he makes his friend."

> (Sunan Abi Dawud 4833)

Question and Answer

Q1. You mentioned something along the lines of curiosity, how certain types of curiosity would lead you to getting into the worst situation than you were in before. So I was wondering what type of curiosity is permissible, and in what situations would it be alright to ask?

A. Maybe I was wrong for using the word curiosity, perhaps, because what I meant in that context of following and obeying Allah (s.w.t.) was different from curiosity.

We may ask about the reason why certain things are made halal and haram. I have a lot of students. I deal with teenagers who are not only inquisitive, but they are bored to death, so they would ask a lot of questions. And I attend to them all the time, because if I left them where would they go? They would go to shaykh Google, and al-Hajj Facebook, and end up getting the worst knowledge ever. So we have to attend to teenagers, especially our children. If we have children, allow them to ask those types of questions, even if they appear stupid or silly. That is why I said no question is considered silly. This is where I missed out, the answer system. When we really do not know why the Prophet (s.a.w.) prohibited certain things, we should not go beyond that. Do not let our curiosity take us beyond what the Prophet mentioned, and what Allah said.

For example, the Prophet (s.a.w.) never mention why cutting the hair from the side is haram. Should we now investigate and do research, go to students at the university and tell them, we need PhD holders to get together to discover the reality of why? We may know, time may come when we discover a reality of why Allah made certain things haram, and anything that was made haram is harmful. That is the basic understanding of what haram is, it is harmful to you. *Riba'* for example. Up until now, people are still engaging in interest and *riba'*, and they keep coming up with these types of questions. Thirty or forty years ago, we did not really know the most logical understanding of why *riba'* is haram. Only recently when people really came up with the damaging results of *riba'*, people started to understand why it is haram. So once we know certain things are haram, avoid it completely, even if we do not know the reason. But, if we are curious, ask, and if the answer is available, *Alḥamdulillāh*.

Curious people have disadvantages. We will get to know a lot when we ask, but how many of the things we know will be applied in our life?

Q2. I would like to ask for some tips on marriage. We know that hypothetically when we get married, either husband or wife will have a lot of expectations, so according to what you talked about, how we need to entail whatever expectations, whatever it is, the end outcome is Allah. So what is the tip to make our expectations less driven by our emotions? Because it is very difficult.

A. No, we made it difficult. Look, Allah (s.w.t.) made it very clear:

$$\text{لَا يُكَلِّفُ ٱللَّهُ نَفْسًا إِلَّا وُسْعَهَا} \ldots ﴿٢٨٦﴾$$

"Allah does not require of any soul more than what it can afford."

(surah al-Baqarah, 2:286)

Allah would not give us a burden, He will give us a *challenge* that we can actually bear, that we are capable of handling. And once we are capable of handling anything, do we think the word 'difficult' will appear in our life? Let's say if you were given a task that you are a master of, would you say it is difficult, or would you say, "it is very challenging, but I can overcome it"? The answer is the latter tight? Why? Because the challenge is within our limits, but sometimes in life, Allah will give us what we can bear, but those things do not satisfy us. So we bring more burden into our lives and we would say it is too difficult. Allah will never place anything upon us, other than what we can actually carry and consume. If we are not satisfied with that, we will go for more, and that is where it would bring more troubles into our life. That is where we lose that balance between handling our activities and emotional connection with each other.

So we actually brought the burden to ourselves. That is why I say, 'live your life simply.' Do not live beyond what we can actually consume. There is a difference between what we want and what we need. So if we can list down what we need and work around that, then we will live a happy life, *wallah*. But if we run after what we want, there is no limit. We will keep bringing burdens into our lives.

Q3. I have a question on sincerity. Let's say I help someone out and of course I did not expect anything in return. But, can I expect Allah will help me, help make it easy for me in any situation?

A. Absolutely. But, do not regret not getting anything in return. If your intention on helping people so Allah can help you out, Allah will definitely, a million percent help you.

"Allah's Messenger (ﷺ) said, Allah said, 'O son of Adam! Spend, and I shall spend on you.'"

(Ṣaḥīḥ al-Bukhari 5352)

Spending here means provision of all sorts. As I mentioned, there is a difference between what we want and what we need. Allah (s.w.t.) will always help us get what we need—the necessity in life. That is why Allah gave us the Qur'an and the sunnah. What we need to attain salvation and go to *Jannah*.

Prophet (s.a.w.) said in a hadith:

وَحَدَّثَنِي عَنْ مَالِكٍ، أَنَّهُ بَلَغَهُ أَنَّ رَسُولَ اللَّهِ صلى الله عليه وسلم قَالَ « تَرَكْتُ فِيكُمْ أَمْرَيْنِ لَنْ تَضِلُّوا مَا تَمَسَّكْتُمْ بِهِمَا كِتَابَ اللَّهِ وَسُنَّةَ نَبِيِّهِ » .

"Yahya related to me from Malik that he heard that the Messenger of Allah, may Allah bless him and grant him peace, said, 'I have left two matters with you. As long as you hold onto them, you will not go the wrong way. They are the Book of Allah and the sunnah of His Prophet.'"

(Book 46, Ḥadith 3)

That is what we need to hold on to, *Insha'Allāh*. So, help people with that intention, no problem. But do not complain if Allah puts us in trials, tribulations, and difficulties, and proceed to not helping others just because Allah does not help us. Do not ever mistaken Allah's challenges to Him not helping us. Allah may not always give us what we ask for, but only because it is not good for us. He knows better.

Q4. What is the difference between taking the religion seriously or not taking it lightly and not making it difficult?

A. Imagine someone came from a background where Islam is unheard of, or whatever they heard about Islam is very negative. Once they came to a certain country where Islam is more known, and they were introduced to Islam, can they convert to Islam? Yes, of course.

I used to run an organisation in Hong Kong called 'Serving Islam Team', and we witnessed so many people coming to Islam. And I remembered, there were many *daʿi* who would come and tell the brothers and sisters who are interested to hear some information about Islam, that Islam is easy, "Just take the *shahadah*, and everything will be alright. And it will be like a mountain falling off your shoulders, you will feel light. So are you ready? Please repeat after me, '*ʾash-hadu an la ilāha illa Allah, wa ʾash-hadu anna Muḥammadan Rasulu-Allah*.'" These people were very excited, but then all of a sudden the *daʿi* said, "okay, from now on wear hijabs and abayas when you are going out, do not eat pork anymore, remove the tattoos in your arms immediately." This actually makes it difficult for these brothers and sisters, this is how people make religion difficult.

But once we realise that Islam is simple, and Allah's obligatory is simple. we must pray five times a day, on time. And we must prefer the *ibadah* over anything else worldly. That is what not to take Islam lightly means. It means that if our heart is not attached to praying the *sunnah*, that is okay, as long as we perfect our five obligatory prayers. Maybe we do not have the energy for the *sunnah*, then it is okay, leave it for a while.

Like say, for *tahajjud*. People will plan on sleeping early and wake up in the middle of the night to perform tahajjud, that is what people have in mind about *tahajjud*. But *tahajjud* is defined by the Prophet (s.a.w.) as a prayer to be performed any time after isya' until before fajr. So we do not have to sleep first and wake up later to do *tahajjud*, we can actually pray it after isya'. It is only two rak'ah, it is not that difficult. The only question is can we do it? Can we dedicate five minutes of our time to perform the two rak'ah prayers which the Prophet (s.a.w.) mentioned is the best prayers after the obligatory prayers.

"The Messenger of Allah (ﷺ) said: 'The best fasting after the month of Ramadan is the month of Allah, Al-Muharram, and the best prayer is prayer at night (tahajjud prayer)."'

(Sunan an-Nasa'i 1613)

I used to have a *qiyam al-layl* course back in Hong Kong where I dedicated the whole day talking and teaching about *tahajjud*, the next day when I came to my class, I noticed that my own centre was locked from the inside, turns out there were a group of sisters practising *tahajjud* after hearing my class. However, I was confused as to why they were sleeping in my centre instead of going home after the prayer. One of the sisters told me they ended up falling asleep after performing one hundred rak'ah of *tahajjud* prayer and accidentally missed their fajr prayer. So this is what makes people sometimes despise the religion, because we impose on them the optional options as if they are obligatory. Although back then, the people did look at the optional actions as obligatory. Whatever the Prophet (s.a.w.) did, to them that is something of very high value, which should be our attitude. But if we are not there yet, we can take it step by step, maintain the obligations and then go beyond, once we are comfortable with the obligations.

Q5. I am very intrigued to share islamic values, stories, and islamic talk to people, but whenever those thoughts would pop up, I would discard those and leave it in my archive, because I know I am not worthy of sharing it, and I am no ustazah or even close to it, so how should I go about it?

A. See, once we say, "I am not ready", we are already telling our brain who we are. We already limit our own beliefs, our own self. Allah left us with a wealth of information and knowledge to share. If the Prophet (s.a.w.) said, "share one *ayah* (sentence)."

"The Prophet (ﷺ) said,

'Convey (my teachings) to the people even if it were a single sentence,...'"

(Ṣaḥiḥ al-Bukhari 3461)

Even if it is one *ayah*, do we think we are not ready? Do we really think we are not ready to say, "You know that in Islam, our beloved Prophet Muḥammad (s.a.w.) said, 'if I smile in your face, it is actually a charity.', so my dear sister, smile."

I do this with non-muslims a lot, these kind of

tricky jokes that have an Islamic value attached to it. I will also do some friendly competition with my non-muslim brothers. I would sing one song and one Qur'anic verse, and they would have to identify which is the Qur'anic verse from the two. Most of the time, they would identify the correct verse, and then they would be confused as to how they would guess it correctly. This is because the Qur'an is revealed to not only Muslims. It was released to every soul being created by Allah (s.w.t.).

Leonardo Recaldi was one of my friends in the Philippines, in 2005 he passed away, may Allah have mercy on him. I knew him for only three years, during my early state of *da'wah* career coming to Islam. But the story of how this man became a Muslim is amazing. This man was a pastor in a church in the Philippines, and the church sponsored him to go to Saudi Arabia to convert Muslims to Christianity, that was his mission. At the airport, before he even went into the country, he saw a magazine store and saw a sticker on the glass saying, 'read the Qur'an, the Last Testament'. He was a pastor studying the Bible, and we all know that the Bible is divided into two; the Old Testament and the New Testament, there is no such thing as the Last Testament. When he saw the statement, it intrigued him, so he went to the store and asked the seller, the seller told him it is the book of the Muslims. Thinking that he came to Saudi Arabia to convert Muslims to Christianity, he decided to buy the Qur'an, to study and understand it. He read it for eight months on his own, and became a Muslim on his own. One day, he went to the *masjid* to pray, at the time, nobody knew he was already a Muslim. After praying, he went to the back of the *masjid* to drink *zamzam* water, because in Saudi Arabia, they always provide *zamzam* water in every masjid. As he was drinking, an *imam* came and asked him who he was, because he had never seen him before. When he introduced himself as Leonardo, the *imam* asked if he was a Muslim. He answered, "yes, I just embraced Islam a few months ago by myself." The *imam* then told him he had to take the *shahadah* in front of everybody, and he did. They celebrated, and he later changed his name to Ahmad Ricaldi. He travelled Saudi to almost every city to talk to the Filipino community, and thousands of people became a Muslim because of this man. Thousands of people in the Philippines became Muslims too, because of him, *Masha'Allāh*. He wrote books, he produced videos, even when video at that time was very difficult to achieve. But this man, he did it, he was in the game of *da'wah*, a few years later he passed away.

Now who will gain the rewards of those thousands of people who became Muslims on the Day of Judgment? Which man will get the maximum reward on the Day of Judgment because of the effort of Ahmad Ricaldi? The man who put the sticker. He just took a simple initiative to introduce people to Islam indirectly. So if we are a shy person, if we do not feel comfortable talking in public, maybe an indirect way of *da'wah* can be done. This magazine salesman, he may have never met Ahmad Ricaldi ever again after that encounter, he may have never heard of what happened to him, but he will see his reward on the Day of Judgment, because of the little sticker.

We never know what kind of ways that would attract people to Islam, so do whatever it takes to convey the message, in whatever methodology. All will do, *Insha'Allāh*.

Q6. How do I overcome the feeling of fear that stops me from doing certain things? Eg: fear of not being happy in a marriage or divorce, so I stop wanting to get married.

A. You must read my book 'My Wheelchair', because in that book I spoke about several types of fear that we go through, and some of them is fear of same issue happening again in the future, or the fear of unknown in general. And I came to the conclusion that if the problem that I went through was my problem, if I was the one who caused whatever happened in my life, that just means that I am a human being. I made peace with myself that if I make that mistake, if I was the reason why I was bedridden for a year, I am a human being. I made a mistake, but I still have to go on with my life. But if it was not my fault, then why should I grieve? Why should I torture myself?

So those who went through a divorce experiences or issues related to domestic violence, which led to divorce and the like. I would like to remind you of one thing, my brothers and sisters, *SubḥanAllāh*, if you do not have any intention to harm your spouse, but that is what you got, congratulations. Because the amount of reward that Allah (s.w.t.) will add into your account is immeasurable. But, there is a difference between being patient upon the torture and the violence, and being foolish to stay in such a relationship. I want to be very clear about this. Because that is what we all heard, "be patient," despite seeing marks and bruises in their body. That is foolishness, not patience. There are limits, and we have to draw lines that if these things happen, there is no way forward.

So if you do not intend any harm from your spouse, but that is what you got, then remember, it is not your fault. In fact, Allah (s.w.t.) will reward you. But closing the door of marriage now is a bigger sin in action. There is a story in a hadith on marriage:

Narrated Anas bin Malik:

"A group of three men came to the houses of the wives of the Prophet (ﷺ) asking how the Prophet (ﷺ) worshipped (Allah), and when they were informed about that, they considered their worship insufficient and said, 'Where are we from the Prophet (ﷺ) as his past and future sins have been forgiven.' Then one of them said, 'I will offer the prayer throughout the night forever.' The other said, 'I will fast throughout the year and will not break my fast.' The third said, 'I will keep away from the women and will not marry forever.' Allah's Messenger (ﷺ) came to them and said, 'Are you the same people who said so-and-so? By Allah, I am more submissive to Allah and more afraid of Him than you; yet I fast and break my fast, I do sleep and I also marry women. So he who does not follow my tradition in religion, is not from me (not one of my followers).'"

(Ṣaḥiḥ al-Bukhari 5063)

The Prophet said, فَمَـنْ رَغِـبَ عَـنْ سُـنَّتِي فَلَيْـسَ مِـن "whosoever deviated from my sunnah, my path, they do not belong to me". Also ask yourself, "how will I cater to my needs?" How can we feed from our desires that Allah created for us? How can we cope with those? So do not just block the doors completely, you can take time to heal, once you are ready, *InshàAllāh*, you can start that life of yours. May Allah protect us all.

Q7. People would always say, "to become successful, you need to step out of your comfort zone", but every time I tried to, I would always feel uncomfortable and I feel empty inside. What should I do about it?

A.   Stepping out of our comfort zone should not leave us empty inside. Yes, even though it is hard and requires extra effort to step out of the comfort zone, but at the end, it will be fulfilling. It will give us some sort of fulfilment and achievement at the end. If we did not feel fulfilled in the beginning, then start looking back at our passion. What are we passionate about? Maybe those things are not our niche, not the area that we feel belonged.

I advised you to read a book called 'The One Thing' by Gary W. Keller. He mentioned about this, he said, "most of the time we hook ourselves up with a lot of activities, a lot of things that we want to achieve, only to fall short and achieve nothing. Because we have divided our focus on lots of things. Rather if we want to be successful, try to spot the area that we love the most, the area that lights us up, keep us awake, and focus on that alone." Hopefully, that will bring you some sort of fulfilment, *Insha'Allāh.*